Understanding
Reading and Writing
Research

Understanding Reading and Writing Research

MICHAEL L. KAMIL
University of Illinois at Chicago

JUDITH A. LANGER
Stanford University

TIMOTHY SHANAHAN
University of Illinois at Chicago

Allyn and Bacon, Inc.
BOSTON · LONDON · SYDNEY · TORONTO

Series Editor: Susanne F. Canavan
Production Administrator: Jane Schulman
Editorial/Production Services: B & W Hutchinsons

Library of Congress Cataloging in Publication Data

Kamil, Michael L.
  Understanding reading and writing research.

  Includes bibliographies and index.
  1. Education—Research—Methodology. 2. Educational statistics.
3. Educational surveys. 4. Language arts—Research—
Methodology. I. Langer, Judith A.   II. Shanahan, Timothy.
III. Title.

LB1028.5.K24 1985   370'.7'8   84–20392
ISBN 0–205–08423–0

Printed in the United States of America.
10 9 8 7 6 5 4 3 2 1 90 89 88 87 86 85

Dedication

This book is dedicated to our teachers and students—past, present, and future—all of whom have caused us to question what we know.

We wish to express our appreciation for the help, inspiration, and encouragement given to us by Margaret Quinlin. Without her, this book would have been far more difficult to create.

We also thank Susanne Canavan and Hiram Howard for their help and extreme patience in making certain this project came to fruition.

Table of Contents

Preface

The surest avenue to improvement of educational practice will occur through the application of knowledge derived from careful research. Of course, everyone knows some successful teacher or administrator who has very little knowledge of research findings. Possibly you are one of those persons who just instinctively seems to know what to do in many situations. Talent is valuable, but research makes it possible for all to understand what makes talented teachers successful. Research helps us understand the key elements of successful learning and teaching, so educational applications can accomplish the widest possible effects.

This text will help the reader understand reading and writing research. Research in these closely allied areas examines a wide variety of problems, with a broad range of techniques, from many different perspectives. Knowledge in these areas will help practitioners come to terms with many of the techniques and perspectives of reading and writing research, so they can recognize and evaluate the relevance and validity of findings and apply them accordingly in their instructional situation.

We believe improvement in educational practice must come from careful use of research done in the settings in which teaching and learning take place. Many educators find it difficult to conduct the large-scale research necessary for program implementation and instructional change.

However, there is usually a large body of research literature on most educational methods and practices, and it is useful to consult this literature so trial-and-error can be minimized or eliminated from decision making. There are no guarantees that the answers drawn from available research will match the problems in any specific situation or that the application of available answers will produce perfect results. This is true because research is a continuing endeavor; answers are obtained in slow, methodical, and often unpredictable ways. This volume will help educators locate, read, and understand the possibilities—and limitations—of reading and writing research.

Our purpose is not to explain how to *do* research. Doing sophisticated research takes time, effort, and experience. It can be as much a full-time occupation as any other educational activity. Nonetheless, if this is your interest, many sources are available to help you learn more about doing research. We hope that this volume will encourage nonresearchers to understand and use research. If we also stimulate your curiosity about how to do research, we will be even more pleased.

To benefit from this volume, it will be helpful to have had an introduction to statistics. This is not an absolute requirement, since each statistical concept will be explained when it is used for the first time. However, in the space allotted for each of the sections, we cannot give exhaustive treatments of statistical topics. Should you need or desire to learn more about any of these topics, a list of more detailed and advanced sources is provided. After reading these chapters, you should have acquired enough background to pursue most topics on your own.

We have categorized research literature primarily on the basis of its underlying methodology. It is not possible to judge whether one of these methods or types of research is better than another. Each asks different questions, usually about slightly different circumstances. We have illustrated representative questions and circumstances for each type through selected examples. As you read these chapters, you should seek additional examples of studies and apply the questions and analyses on your own. You will find that, while the studies differ, the same basic analyses apply.

We have devoted a chapter to each method; however, these methods are not equally represented in research literature. At present, the literature is weighted more heavily with experimental studies. Nonetheless, ethnographic techniques are fast becoming a popular and useful tool in the study of classrooms, teaching, and learning.

We have made the selection of studies as utilitarian as possible, including examples of both writing and reading research. In some instances, examples of specific research techniques are limited to one particular area. Thus, some chapters may emphasize reading or writing more than the other. As new studies become available in different methodologies, readers should use these opportunities to apply what they have learned. Practice is a major key to being able to read, understand, and interpret research.

PUBLICATION OF RESEARCH

Some cautions about published research are in order. The authority of the written word exists in the field of research, as in other fields. Findings that are *published* as opposed to those that are simply *presented* or *reported* to some group without external review and evaluation often carry greater weight, even if they are shown later to be in error. This is true not only because the published work is more widely available, but also because it is more apt to be reviewed objectively by various authorities.

For this reason, it is important that the reader be able to distinguish between two kinds of research journals: *refereed* and *nonrefereed*. A nonrefereed journal publishes articles that have not been examined for quality of scholarship by a review board. Some nonrefereed journals publish invited or commissioned articles; others publish all of the papers submitted. The details of submission and selection procedures can be found in each issue of the journal.

In contrast, a refereed journal contains papers that are published only after they have been examined and judged by other researchers. A refereed journal can be identified by looking for the list of members of an editorial advisory board or a review board, which should be published in every issue.

When articles are submitted, the editor of the journal asks reviewers (usually experts in the particular research area) to critique the manuscript. This is usually done "blindly." That is, the author's name is withheld from the reviewers so the researcher's identity does not influence the evaluation. If the work is judged to be of high quality, free from error, it is accepted for publication. However, quality is not the only criterion. Sometimes articles are selected on the basis of interest or relevance for a given audience. Thus, journals limit the domain in which they will publish articles.

Another matter is that certain research problems are not always of popular interest. Research is performed in those areas in which researchers are interested and for which they can obtain funding. There are no guarantees that one study is better or more important than another. However, over the long term, we accumulate a comprehensive body of knowledge on which we can depend.

Remember these cautions as you read the research reported in journals and other sources. What you find may not be precisely what you want or need. Therefore, you must be able to work with what is provided. This text will give you the tools to do just that. It is up to you to use them.

PLAN FOR THE TEXT

Chapter 1 examines similarities and differences in reading and writing research. Chapter 2 presents examples of strategies to use when reading research reports. Although there can be much variability in report formats, the examples provided represent most of what you can expect to find.

Individual research traditions and methods are explained and illustrated in Chapters 3 through 8. These methods have been categorized as ethnographic, descriptive, correlational, experimental, and multivariate.

Chapter 9 discusses the problems of synthesizing, reviewing, and applying results from several different research studies. And Appendix A lists journals and other sources of information to help in the search for research reports. Finally, Appendix B provides a table of critical values of the Pearson product-moment correlation coefficient.

Acknowledgments

The authors would like to thank the following for permission to use segments of their research reports as examples:

Chapter 2

Dyson, A. H. (1983). The role of oral language in early writing processes. *Research in the Teaching of English, 17*(1), 1–30. Reprinted with the permission of the National Council of Teachers of English.

Gearhart, M., & Newman, D. (1980). Learning to draw a picture: The social context of an individual activity. *Discourse Processes, 3*(2), 169–184. Reprinted with permission of Ablex Publishing Corporation.

Markman, E. (1977). Realizing that you don't understand: A preliminary investigation. *Child Development, 48,* 986–992. Reprinted with permission of the author and the Society for Research in Child Development, Inc.

Chapter 3

Cunningham, J., & Cunningham, P. (1978). Validating a limited-cloze procedure. *Journal of Reading Behavior, 10,* 211–213. Reprinted with permission of the National Reading Conference.

Hanna, G. (1979). An improved design for examining the importance of context dependence. *Journal of Reading Behavior, 11,* 329–337. Reprinted with permission of the National Reading Conference.

McCormick, C., & Samuels, S. J. (1979). Word recognition by second graders: The unit of perception and interrelationships among accuracy, latency, and comprehension. *Journal of Reading Behavior, 11,* 107–118. Reprinted with permission of the National Reading Conference.

Ryan, E. B., McNamara, S., & Kenney, M. (1977). Linguistic awareness and reading performance among beginning readers. *Journal of Reading Behavior, 9,* 399–400. Reprinted with permission of the National Reading Conference.

Tierney, R., Bridge, C., & Cera, M. (1978–79). The discourse processing operations of children. *Reading Research Quarterly, 14,* 539–573. Reprinted with permission of the authors and the International Reading Association.

Chapter 4

Durkin, D. (1978–79). What classroom observations reveal about reading comprehension instruction. *Reading Research Quarterly, 14*(4), 483–533. Reprinted with permission of the author and the International Reading Association.

Chapter 5

Heath, S. B. (1982). Questioning at home and at school: A comparative study. From *Doing the Ethnography of Schooling,* edited by George Spindler. Copyright © 1982 by CBS College Publishing. Reprinted by permission of Holt, Rinehart and Winston, CBS College Publishing.

Chapter 6

Christopherson, S. (1978). Effects of knowledge of semantic roles on recall of written prose. *Journal of Reading Behavior, 10,* 249–256. Reprinted with permission of the National Reading Conference.

Chapter 7

Carnine, D., Kameenui, E., & Woolfson, W. (1982). Training of textual dimension related to text-based inferences. *Journal of Reading Behavior, 14,* 335–340. Reprinted with permission of the National Reading Conference.

Freedman, S., & Calfee, R. (1983). From "Holistic Assessment of Writing: Experimental Design and Cognitive Theory" by Sarah Warshauer Freedman and Robert C. Calfee in *RESEARCH IN WRITING: Principles and Methods* edited by Peter Mosenthal, Lynne Tamor and Sean A. Walmsley. Copyright © 1983 by Longman Inc. Reprinted by permission of Longman Inc., New York.

Chapter 8

DeSoto, J. L., & DeSoto, C. B. (1983). Relationship of reading achievement to verbal processing abilities. *Journal of Educational Psychology, 75,* 116–127. Copyright © 1983 by the American Psychological Association. Reprinted/adapted by permission of the publisher and author.

Hiebert, E. H., Englert, C. S., & Brennan, S. (1983). Awareness of text structure in recognition and production of expository discourse. *Journal of Reading Behavior, 15*(4), 63–79. Reprinted with permission of the National Reading Conference.

Chapter 9

Guthrie, J., Seifert, M., & Mosberg, L. (1983). Research synthesis in reading: Topics, audiences, and citation rates. *Reading Research Quarterly, 19*(1), 16–27. Reprinted with permission of the authors and the International Reading Association.

Ladas, H. (1980). Summarizing research: A case study. *Review of Educational Research, 50,* 597–624. Copyright © 1980, American Educational Research Association, Washington, D.C.

Moore, D., & Readence, J. (1980). A meta-analysis of the effect of graphic organizers on learning from text. In M. Kamil (ed.), *Perspectives in reading research and instruction* (Twenty-ninth yearbook). Washington, D.C.: The National Reading Conference.

Sticht, T., Beck, L., Hauke, R., Kleiman, G., & James, J. (1974). *Auding and reading.* Alexandria, VA: HumRRO (Human Resources Research Organization). Reprinted with permission of HumRRO.

Appendix B

We are grateful to the Literary Executor of the late Sir Ronald A. Fisher, F.R.S., to Dr. Frank Yates, F.R.S., and to Longman Group Ltd., London, for permission to reprint Table VII from their book *Statistical Tables for Biological, Agricultural and Medical Research* (6th Edition, 1974).

Chapter 1

What is Reading and Writing Research?

Research is the systematic attempt to explain the world around us. It is a continuing endeavor that takes many forms in many different domains. In this chapter, we will discuss and illustrate the techniques, content, and forms of research in reading. We will also see how some general research principles apply to studies in both reading and writing.

Reading research, as we know it today, has its roots in psychological experiments conducted in Germany and France in the late nineteenth century (for instance, see Wundt 1850). By the early part of the twentieth century, an effort to understand the underlying components was begun by such pioneers as William S. Gray (1919).

Until the 1960s, the major research efforts in reading focussed on identifying subskills. Once the parts were identified and taught systematically, learning to read was expected to be the natural result.

Although writing instruction has been long established (in fact, some of the instructional concepts we use today are derived from Aristotle), research to understand or explain the writing process began on a large scale only during the past decade. The early focus of writing research was more meaning based and holistic in scope (Shaunessy 1977; Britton 1970). Only recently have writing researchers begun to examine the subprocesses in writing (Hayes and Flower 1980).

At one level, reading and writing research do not differ very much from research in other fields. At another level, however, we will see that the research questions posed, as well as the methodologies used to answer these questions, reflect the special characteristics of the domains themselves. What, then, differentiates reading and writing research from other research?

Contemporary research in reading and writing is a rich mixture of influences from cognitive and physiological psychology, linguistics, anthropology, computer science, social psychology, learning theory, and educational practice. These influences range from the most abstract, theoretical points of view to the most practical, applied knowledge. Some reading and writing research is aimed at understanding the basic nature of the reading process. Such efforts include the generation of models and theories of the reading process. Summaries of much of the earlier work in modeling and theory construction are found in Singer and Ruddell (1976) and Davis (1971). The continued popularity of this research is seen in recent work by Carver (1977–78), Gough, Alford, and Holley-Wilcox (1979), Hayes and Flower (1980), Bereiter and Scardamalia (1982), and many others.

Another goal of reading and writing research is to improve educational practices in classrooms and other instructional settings. These efforts include studies that unobtrusively observe behaviors in natural instructional settings, as well as those that conduct highly controlled manipulations of variables affecting reading and reading instruction. Major efforts have been mounted at the institutes, laboratories, and centers funded by federal monies to accomplish this task in a systematic manner.

BASIC AND APPLIED
READING RESEARCH

The goal of educational research is to gain knowledge that can help us make predictions, manipulate events, or make changes in environments that affect learning and literacy, within both school and nonschool settings. Because educational research is so diverse, it is helpful to distinguish between two broad categories: *basic* and *applied* research.

Basic research is the attempt to *explain* some part of the events in the world around us. It endeavors to develop knowledge that is consistent with or leads to a theory. At any given time, basic research may have little or no applicability to specific situations beyond those in the immediate research area. If we develop a comprehensive theory, we will be able to explain the events within the domain of that theory. Namely, we will be able to specify when and why events occur. Obviously, the closer a theory comes to being complete, the more readily we can apply it to large segments of the real world.

Applied research involves the use of basic research findings or theory to solve specific, real-world problems. Kerlinger (1977) gives the following example:

> Suppose a theory of learning has been found to be empirically valid, and rather successfully explains the learning of concepts. . . . It may or may not have implications for teaching concepts to children. . . . A

teaching expert now devises a method of teaching concepts based on the theory. He is an engineer, a technologist. . . . [H]e may test the efficacy of his method using techniques devised by scientists. His research is applied research which is in this case inspired by the original basic research. (1977, 5–6)

Kerlinger points out a paradox in talking about strictly applied research. He asserts that applied research is the application of existing technology to problems at hand. In the field of reading, it is rare that practitioners from either end of the basic-applied continuum interact to generate mutually interesting research problems.

Day-to-day educational problems or questions often become applied issues because of the need and desire for immediate answers. Often, however, the answers to these questions cannot be fully determined, because the necessary basic research has not been done. This is why researchers and educators must inform each other and work together, developing appropriate basic research questions and applying those results in appropriate manners in appropriate settings.

The differing vantage points of practitioners and researchers have produced some differences in types of research studies. On the applied end of the continuum is a preponderance of one-time studies or evaluations of individual programs, methods, or techniques. The question in each case is whether one program or method produces better learning than others.

Theoreticians tend to design programs of research studies in which the outcome of each piece bears on the conduct of the next. An organizing framework, point of view, model, or theory usually guides the selection of variables and methodologies. And often, but not always, the outcomes of studies are used as feedback to revise the framework or model governing the research program. Uncertainties about the reliability of data can make researchers feel more confident with logical argument than empirical data.

It is impossible to state that either logic or data is a superior basis for argument. However, exclusive reliance on logic has produced research that seeks to validate models, rather than explore processes. In turn, this has lead to some confusion about appropriate research methodologies. Recent interest in descriptive and ethnographic methods can be attributed, in part, to a lack of confidence that traditional experimental methods will produce results generalizable to real-world settings. (We will treat descriptive research more fully in chapter 4 and ethnographic research in chapter 5.)

RELATING GOALS
TO RESEARCH QUESTIONS

Goals for reading and writing research are quite diverse, reflecting the nature of the subject itself. When one reads research, a primary task is to determine what the research questions will be. These questions can be at the level of attempting to determine basic facts about cognitive processes, or they can be about instructional decisions.

Before researchers can begin to deal with a problem, they must limit their efforts by stating the specific questions they will attempt to answer. These questions serve to guide the research and keep it focussed on the topic at hand. A good research question is precise, unambiguous, and, of course, limited in scope. Without such limits, the research might never be resolved. And if the question is not precise and unambiguous, researchers might study one problem while *thinking* they are studying something else. Removing ambiguity also assures that different researchers will be able to agree that they are working on the same problem.

Research questions may be quite broad in scope—such as What are the student-teacher interactions during instruction?—or they may be more narrow—like What is the effect of repeatedly reading a passage on the ability to answer comprehension questions? As a study progresses, these questions are often refined. Many reports describe several studies or experiments that grew out of a single, original question.

When one reads a research report, the first task should be to determine the research question. One complicating problem arises in experimental studies that have *null hypotheses*, which are different from research questions. A null hypothesis is a device used for statistical reasons; it states, as a hypothesis, that there will be no observed differences in the experiment. In comparison, a research question generally poses the problem without taking a stance about the outcome of the study. (Null hypotheses are discussed in more detail in chapter 6.)

INFLUENCES ON
READING AND WRITING RESEARCH

Three groups shape current trends in reading and writing research. The first is a very diverse *researchers* group, which addresses several interests. Some researchers examine the basic processes of reading or writing, without considering the relevance or applicability of the results to instructional situations. Other researchers look for cognitive or social patterns that affect learning. And still others focus on learning and the development of knowledge, in and out of school settings. What ties these different researchers together is a desire to see how the elements in the educational domain fit together—how they can be explained. Ultimately, they want to know how the educational process works.

The second group that shapes research is the *practitioners* who have direct, day-to-day contact with learners. Because these professionals are always seeking new ideas or answers to problems, they exert a strong force on the questions being asked by many researchers. That is, they prompt evaluation of methods, validation of tests, and identification of crucial variables in instruction. Quite simply, practitioners ask whether research is relevant or directly translatable into practice. Pressure for this kind of relevant research sometimes comes from various funding agencies, which are often more interested in obtaining products or answers to specific questions than increasing basic knowledge.

The final group exerting influence on research is the *translators*, a relatively small but growing group that has some interests in common with both researchers and practitioners. Translators have two tasks: (1) They speculate on the implications of experimental research and theory for instruction; and (2) they point out the need for further research on instructional questions.

Translators often use basic research data to design and perform applied research studies of specific problems. At other times, they try to make informed guesses or predictions based on the best available evidence. In addition, translators synthesize experimental results and generate new instructionally related research problems.

In order to fulfill these purposes, the translator group employs both researchers and practitioners who have interests in improving the teaching and learning of reading and writing. Because of the complex and esoteric nature of contemporary research, translators are becoming increasingly important in helping teachers understand developments in research and in prompting researchers to explore new directions.

RESEARCH IS INFLUENCED BY THEORIES AND MODELS

Three major theoretical orientations characterize or dominate most of reading and writing research.

The first of these is the *bottom-up* or *skills* position. This orientation asserts that the reading process is initiated by information on the page and that the writing process begins with the organization of words, the construction of sentences, and the parsing of sentences. That is, reading is assumed to be initiated from letter units to words, sentences, and then meaning, while writing is assumed to be initiated from within and between sentence information. Examples of these models in reading are found in the work of Gough, Alford, and Holley-Wilcox (1972), LaBerge and Samuels (1974), and Carver (1977–78). In writing, such models are implicit in widely used instructional materials (Warriner and Griffith 1977). Research conducted from this orientation emphasizes skills, subskills, decoding, spelling, mechanics, and the like.

A second position is referred to as *top-down* or *holistic*. According to this position, reading is initiated by informed guesses at the meaning of the text and proceeds through verification of those guesses. Examples of these sorts of reading models are found in the early work of Goodman (1965) and Smith (1971). (Note, however, that Goodman's more recent work is different from that cited here. He suggests that his newer models fall in the interactive category, described next.) From this perspective, writing is assumed to be meaning generated from and focussed on what the writer is saying, has said, and is going to say (Britton 1970). Research conducted from this holistic position emphasizes the global nature of language and the centrality of meaning.

A final approach is called *interactive* or *balanced*. It suggests that reading involves processes that operate *simultaneously* as the reader extracts information by decoding words from the page *and* makes guesses about the meaning of the text. Information from each source facilitates the other until a final meaning is verified. The best example of this sort of model is found in Rumelhart (1977). When research is conducted from this orientation, emphasis is divided appropriately between skills and holistic variables. Hayes and Flower (1980) have a related view of writing as a recursive activity involving planning, translating, and reviewing with an editing subprocess that can interrupt any other subprocess.

These are certainly not the only theoretical positions, since much research tends to be highly eclectic. However, most research is related to one of the three concepts described above. Nonetheless, note that these positions may not be found in pure forms in research studies. More likely, they will represent general dispositions, rather than ironclad foundations for theories, as different theorists focus on different aspects of the reading or writing process. One should always be wary of labels, and these are not exceptions. When used with caution, however, these descriptions provide the proper framework to interpret research by indicating where the theoretical emphasis has been placed.

RESEARCH IS SHAPED
BY THE TYPES OF EXPERIMENTAL DESIGNS USED

Not all research should be designed to yield *explanatory* information. Some effort must be expended to collect *descriptive* data, as well. Often, descriptive or observational data are needed to identify or clarify instructional questions. For example, an investigator studying the most common words in third-grade books would depend on word lists, frequency counts, or sentence grammars, which are the results of descriptive research. But until it is certain that there are measurable and stable differences in these variables, research manipulating them is futile.

Causal explanations—the ability to specify what variables produce specific outcomes under all conditions—are the seldom-attained goal of much educational research. There are, however, many correlational or factor-analytic studies found in reading research, even though no causal inferences can be drawn. Cause-and-effect relationships require experimental designs that allow attribution of effects to (and only to) the manipulated variables. Correlational studies can be very useful when variables cannot be manipulated for dealing with tests or when there are large numbers of measurements involved. (A full treatment of correlational research is given in chapter 3.)

RESEARCH IS SHAPED
BY THE ENVIRONMENT IN WHICH IT IS CONDUCTED

Research may be conducted in the field (a classroom) or in the laboratory (a clinic). It is difficult but not impossible to conduct experimental research in the field. On the other hand, descriptive data are difficult (but, again, not impossible) to collect in a laboratory (see, for instance, Carver 1975–76; Carnine and Carnine 1978).

Experimental research is easiest to conduct in a laboratory, where there is precise control over conditions. However, controlling *all* conditions may lead to results that are not directly usable in other settings. Consequently, there are many research techniques that have been developed for use in educational settings, including descriptive and ethnographic methods. (We will discuss these methods in greater detail in chapters 4 and 5, respectively.)

Different research methods are used in different settings; however, no one method is better than another. In the remainder of this volume, we will demonstrate the use to which the different methods may be put.

RESEARCH METHODOLOGIES:
AN OVERVIEW

In experimental research, one manipulates variables and observes changes in performance. However, many problems in reading and writing cannot be studied this way. For example, it would be unethical to induce reading disability to study the effectiveness of various methods of remediation. Instead, case history methods are often effectively used to study these sorts of problems, as are ethnographic and descriptive techniques.

In a *case history* study, an attempt is made to observe an individual or a group for an extended period of time and, if necessary, to depend on other records for supporting or supplementary data. The value of this type of research is that it allows one to study, in depth, the specific implementations of programs or methods based on other research data. It is a check on the transferability or generalizability of our research results. That is, if we find that a method does not work when we use it in a real situation, we have probably missed an important variable in the other research studies. The potential flaw in this design is that the history is not under the investigator's control. Full and accurate records may not be available; the necessary information may never have been recorded.

Inference of causality in this design will be risky, at best, for several reasons. First, the history of an individual may be unusual. Generalizing to others may thus be risky or inappropriate. Second, extraneous variables may have influenced the treatments administered during the course of the history. If so, no conclusion can be made about the relationship between those treatments and results. Third, not all of the relevant data may have been recorded, or perhaps different techniques of data collection or recording were used during the case history. Finally, the data collection may be biased, since the experimenter is often the only individual responsible for the data.

Despite these potential problems, case histories are often useful in studying a problem or proposed solutions to problems. That is, case histories often provide an accurate view of how an individual (or a group of individuals) reacts in a realistic situation, without intervention by researchers.

Another common method of doing research outside the laboratory is the *correlational* study. (Discussions of research designs and types of variables are found in Popham 1972; Campbell and Stanley 1963; Sullivan 1972; and Resta and Baker 1972.) This technique is common when the variables of interest are not directly manipulable. For instance, the use of good and poor readers as an independent variable produces many correlational studies; the observed differences in performance are correlated with (not necessarily caused by) differences in reading ability. (Correlational methods are discussed in chapter 3.)

Underscore the notion that correlational studies do not strictly allow causal conclusions. However, strong correlations should *suggest* causal relationships, even though correlation does not imply causation. As with case histories, such suggestions have to be verified by other techniques. When regression analyses are used, prediction is possible, but explanation still does not result. This is true for multivariate analyses: What changes is the number of variables that can be accounted for in prediction and theprecision of the predictions. (Multivariate studies are discussed in chapter 8.)

Factor-analytic studies are yet another way of dealing with descriptive data. Factor analysis enjoyed greater popularity in the past than it does today (Davis 1968). However, many problems can still be studied by using factor analysis. For instance, attitudes are particularly amenable to study by this method. While factor analysis does not allow causal inferences, it is valuable for work in difficult problem areas. For example, these techniques can show which of many variables acting on a situation are most important and which may be largely irrelevant. (These techniques are dealt with in chapter 8.)

Historically, the *two-group* study has been the most common experimental design. It operates quite simply: One group is given a treatment, and the other functions as a control group, receiving either nothing or some irrelevant condition for comparison.

This basic design has been extended to produce what is perhaps the most common experimental design in use today, the *factorial* design. In a factorial design, two or more variables (or factors) are manipulated at the same time, in the same study. All values of each variable are combined with all values of the other variables to produce treatment combinations to be administered.

On one level, this is only a more complex form of the two-group design. However, the use of factorial designs allows the effects of several variables to be studied simultaneously. In addition, we can study the interaction among factors, those conditions that occur when variables act differently in combination than when they are observed in isolation. The greater the number of variables manipulated at once in a given setting, the more natural the situation will be. The desirability of this *ecological validity* is carefully shown by Bronfenbrenner (1976). (Experimental studies are discussed in chapters 7 and 8.)

For a long time, psychological researchers have recognized the difficulties inherent in using group data in analyses. Some researchers in learning have advocated intensively studying single (or small numbers of) subjects across an extended range of time and/or behaviors. Noted among those in experimental psychology is Skinner (1957).

Perhaps the most prevalent paradigm in reading research using this single/small number of subjects (N) methodology has been that of *miscue analysis* (for instance, Goodman 1965). Most miscue studies do analysis of extensive data collected in individual sessions with, at most, a few readers. A primary argument for this methodology is that the relationships among responses are often as important as their content. In writing, Graves (1975) conducted extensive small-N research, tracing the writing development of primary schoolchildren. Because only a few subjects are involved, the collected data can be intensively analyzed.

There are potential risks involved in doing research with single-N/small-N samples. Foremost among these is the potential for studying nonrepresentative individuals. Conclusions based on nonrepresentative data are inappropriate for general applications. The smaller the sample, the greater the risk of error. Interpretations based on such data have to be viewed with care. Thus, the researcher is especially obligated to describe the subjects as carefully and thoroughly as possible.

Small-sample paradigms necessitate repeated measures, and both the benefits and disadvantages of collecting repeated measures are involved. Repeated measures allow individuals to serve as their own controls, reducing the variance and increasing the precision of the analysis.

However, when repeated measures are used, contrast effects may arise. That is, subjects may react differentially to the various treatments only because they realize the treatments are different. In addition, repeated measures are subject to practice and fatigue effects, further limiting the generalizability of repeated measures data.

A variant of single-/small-N designs is the *time series*. In this type of study, measurements are made many times, before and after administration of a treatment. Changes in performance can be observed over time and as a function of the application of the treatment. It is not necessary to have a small or single N to use a time series design. However, the extensive data collection required by this design makes it less practical to use large groups.

More sophisticated designs for experimental and quasi-experimental studies in reading are available. The need for these more complex designs has come from two sources. On the one hand, researchers have realized the inadequacies of some conventional methods of collecting data. For example, Bronfenbrenner's (1976) notions of ecological validity have necessitated collection of much more data than was traditionally required. Moreover, contemporary experiments require greater effort in data reduction than in actual data analysis, as any glance at reading or writing research journals will indicate. The use of computers has made the analysis of large amounts of data in complex designs a routine matter.

RESEARCH CAN BE SHAPED BY THE MANIPULATIONS OF THE VARIABLES

Research often can be characterized by the number of factors manipulated. Much reading research has involved manipulating only a single variable. However, researchers increasingly use designs that manipulate several variables simultaneously. This reflects the realization that clusters of variables have to be studied to arrive at a thorough description or explanation of the reading process. A complete description is, by definition, ecologically valid. The growing use of complex designs with a larger number of variables also reflects the growing sophistication among reading researchers. As doctoral training places increased emphasis on research sophistication, even greater reliance on computer-aided analysis will make the use of these designs much more manageable.

Other research performs *evaluative manipulations*. In these cases, a single value of a variable is used to determine whether there is some effect on behavior. Examples might be in test development or in testing a single teaching method or technique. These studies once dominated reading research but seem to be less prevalent now than some years ago.

Finally, there are studies of studies, or *meta-analyses*. In meta-analyses, studies that have manipulated the same or similar variables are examined to determine the amount of agreement among the studies and to estimate the size of effects that can be expected. These meta-analyses are not primary manipulations of variables. Instead, they are attempts to analyze the results of other studies to see what it is that can be assumed to be true about reading and reading processes. (These issues will be discussed in chapter 9.)

TYPES OF VARIABLES
IN READING AND WRITING RESEARCH

Three major classes of variables can be identified. The first is the class of *instructional* variables, including, among others, instructional format, amount of time on task, and type of materials. Topic, knowledge, and purpose of materials have become predominant in current research. This class of variable is a mixture of traditional types, like amount of time on task, and instructional presentation, as well as less traditional types, like teacher beliefs or other aspects of teacher competence (Harste and Burke 1977; Duffy and Metheny 1979).

The second group is the *reader/writer/learner* variables. In turn, this group is divided into individual variables, like language and language development, cognitive processes, and cognitive development, along with more global variables, like self-concept or socioeconomic and cultural factors.

The final group of variables may be classified as *environmental*, which includes such factors as classroom design and organization. Also involved are a number of naturalistic variables dealing with student/teacher interactions.

IN SUMMARY

In this chapter, we have provided a brief overview of the goals and constraints posed in various kinds of reading and writing research. This research has explained a good deal about reading and writing, much of which is very useful for educational decision making. However, to interpret research reports, one must understand research methodology, its advantages and limitations. The methodology used to conduct a study has a logic of its own, an internal logic so strong that it affects the design of the experiment, the procedures used, the data gathered, the analyses undertaken, and the way in which the research is reported. Finally, an understanding of research methodology will help readers know what information to look for and how to avoid misinterpretations. These issues will be discussed in the next chapter.

REFERENCES

Anderson, R. C., Spiro, R. J., & Montague, W. E. (1977). *Schooling and the acquisition of knowledge*. Hillsdale, NJ: Erlbaum.

Bereiter, C., & Scardamalia, M. (1982). From conversation to composition: The role of instruction in developmental processes. In R. Glaser (Ed.), *Advances in instructional psychology* (Vol. 2). Hillsdale, NJ: Erlbaum.

Britton, J. (1970). *Language and learning*. London: Penguin Books.

Bronfenbrenner, U. (1976). The experimental ecology of education. *Educational Researcher, 5,* 5–15.

Campbell, D. T., & Stanley, J. C. (1963). *Experimental and quasi-experimental designs for research.* Chicago: Rand-McNally.

Carnine, L., & Carnine, D. (1978). Determining the relative decoding difficulty of three types of simple regular words. *Journal of Reading Behavior, 10,* 440–441.

Carver, R. P. (1975–76). Measuring prose difficulty using the rauding scale. *Reading Research Quarterly, 11,* 660–685.

Carver, R. P. (1977–78). Toward a theory of reading comprehension and rauding. *Reading Research Quarterly, 13,* 8–63.

Carver, R. P. (1978). Sense and nonsense about generalizing to a language population. *Journal of Reading Behavior, 10,* 25–33.

Davis, F. B. (1971). Research in comprehension in reading. *Reading Research Quarterly, 3,* 499–545.

Cooper, C., & Odell, L. (1978). *Research on composing.* Urbana, IL: NCTE.

Davis, F. B. (Ed.). (1971). *The literature of research in reading with emphasis on models.* New Brunswick, NJ: Graduate School of Education, Rutgers University.

Duffy, G. G., & Metheny, W. (1979). The development of an instrument to measure teacher beliefs about reading. In M. L. Kamil & A. J. Moe (Eds.), *Reading research: Studies and applications* (Twenty-eighth Yearbook of the National Reading Conference, pp. 218–222). Clemson, SC: The National Reading Conference.

Gibson, E. J., & Levin, H. (1975). *The psychology of reading.* Cambridge, MA: MIT Press.

Goodman, K. S. (1965). Analysis of oral reading miscues: Applied psycholinguistics. *Reading Research Quarterly, 1,* 9–30.

Gough, P. B., Alford, J. A., Jr., & Holley-Wilcox, P. (1979). Words and contexts. In M. L. Kamil & A. J. Moe (Eds.), *Reading research: Studies and applications* (Twenty-eighth Yearbook of the National Reading Conference, pp. 72–75). Clemson, SC: The National Reading Conference.

Graves, D. (1975). An examination of the writing processes of seven year old children. *Research in the teaching of English, 9,* 227–241.

Gray, W. S. (1919). Principles of method in teaching reading as derived from scientific investigations. *National Society for the Study of Education yearbook 18, Part II.* Bloomington, IL: Public School Book Company.

Harste, J. C., & Burke, C. (1977). A new hypothesis for reading teacher research: Both the *teaching* and *learning* of reading are theoretically based. In P. D. Pearson (Ed.), *Reading: Theory, research and practice* (Twenty-sixth Yearbook of the National Reading Conference, pp. 32–40). Clemson, SC: The National Reading Conference.

Hayes, J. R., & Flower, L. S. (1980). Identifying the organization of writing processes. In L. W. Gregg & E. R. Steinberg (Eds.), *Cognitive processes in writing.* Hillsdale, NJ: Erlbaum.

Kamil, M. L. (1978). Models of reading: What are the implications for instruction in comprehension. In S. Pflaum-Connor (Ed.), *Aspects of reading education* (pp. 63–88). Berkeley, CA: McCutcheon.

Kerlinger, F. N. (1977). The influence of research on educational practice. *Educational Researcher, 6,* 5–12.

LaBerge, D., & Samuels, S. J. (1974). Toward a theory of automatic information processing in reading. *Cognitive Psychology, 6,* 293–323.

Marshall; N., & Glock, M. (1978–79). Comprehension of connected discourse: A study into the relationships between the structure of text and information recalled. *Reading Research Quarterly, 14,* 10–56.

Pearson, P. D., & Johnson, D. J. (1978). *Teaching reading comprehension.* New York: Holt, Rinehart and Winston.

Pearson, P. D., & Kamil, M. L. (1977–78). What hath Carver raud? A reaction to Carver's 'Toward a theory of reading comprehension and rauding.' *Reading Research Quarterly, 13,* 92–115.

Popham, W. J. (1972). *Simplified design for school research.* New York: American Book.

Resta, P. E., & Baker, R. L. (1972). *Selecting variables for educational research.* New York: American Book.

Rumelhart, D. (1977). Toward an interactive model of reading. In S. Dornic (Ed.), *Attention and performance VI.* Hillsdale, NJ: Erlbaum.

Shaunessy, M. P. (1977). *Errors and expectations.* New York: Oxford University Press.

Shaver, J. P., & Norton, R. S. (1980). Randomness and replication in ten years of the *American Educational Research Journal. Educational Researcher, 9,* 9–16.

Singer, H., & Ruddell, R. B. (Eds.). (1976). *Theoretical models and processes of reading* (2nd ed.). Newark, DE: International Reading Association.

Skinner, B. F. (1957). The experimental analysis of behavior. *American Scientist, 45,* 343–371.

Smith, F. (1971). *Understanding reading.* New York: Holt, Rinehart and Winston.

Sullivan, H. J. (1972). *Classifying and interpreting educational research studies.* New York: American Book.

Tierney, R. J., Bridge, C. A., & Cera, M. J. (1978–79). The discourse processing operations of children. *Reading Research Quarterly, 14,* 539–573.

Warriner, J. E., & Griffith, F. (1977). *English grammar and composition: Complete course.* New York: Harcourt Brace Jovanovich.

Wundt, W. (1850). *Volker-psychologie die sprache* (Vol. 1). Leipzig: W. Engelmann.

Chapter 2

How to Read a Research Report

The structure of a research report is logically derived from the particular research methodology used in the study being reported. Knowing the underlying "rules" of differing methodologies can increase the likelihood that informed readers will understand the reports they read; they will know what kind of information to look for, where to look for it, and what special language is employed. Expectations about the format and content can free the reader to focus on the specific ideas in each new report by fitting the reported information into an expected framework. This framework can assist readers in synthesizing, evaluating, and comparing research reports.

MAJOR RESEARCH ORIENTATIONS

Although most educational researchers are interested in how people behave (and learn), their conceptual orientations are often quite different. And although the author's orientation may seem obscure to the inexperienced report reader, it is the place to begin when reading a report for the first time. Where is this researcher coming from? is a critical question to ask, because once answered, expectations about the nature and shape of the report begin to fall into place. The reader begins to have an idea of *what* to look for, and *where*.

Two basic orientations underly most reading and writing research, reflecting different views of how people learn. One group of researchers, whose views are more closely based in experimentalist traditions, regard behavior as essentially componential. They feel that aspects of behavior are best studied if they are separated out for very close observation, manipulation, and analysis in order to understand better how that particular piece of behavior operates within the whole learning pattern. The other group of researchers, whose views are more closely derived from anthropological or naturalistic traditions, view behavior in a more holistic manner. They view learning as occurring within a natural social and environmental context. Moreover, they believe that when any aspect of that natural context is changed or removed, the behavior itself is changed. Therefore, aspects of behavior can only be studied within the entire behavioral context, in its natural setting.

Research emanating from either of these traditions will be quite different in conceptualization, in assumptions, in the manner in which data are collected, in how the data are interpreted, and in how they are eventually reported.

Assume that we are interested in learning more about the comprehension monitoring behaviors of first-grade children. We will use a research report by Ellen Markman, an experimentalist, as an example. In her report, "Realizing That You Don't Understand: A Preliminary Investigation," Markman (1977) provided instructions for youngsters to play a game and do a magic trick, but deliberately deleted information needed for readers to understand what to do. First- through third-graders were presented with the instructions and asked to help the researcher determine the adequacy of the instructions. The task was individually administered to each child. The focus of the data gathering was clearly on the task itself, on the behavior of the children when completing the task and answering the probing questions, or both. The unit of analysis was based on the students' abilities to answer the comprehension probes.

The report reader can infer the experimental bias of this study from the author's description of how the natural monitoring behaviors that children ordinarily use in real life was manipulated or changed in some way by the task. More change would be expected to occur if the children had visited the researcher in a university laboratory or the vacant nurse's office, and less change if the children had been asked to complete the task as part of a whole class activity. The goal of the study was to analyze how children become aware of their comprehension failures; the study assumed that the findings would typify the behaviors of other first- through third-graders. Research of this sort frequently assumes that examinations of students' responses to researcher's questions can tell something about students' abilities to monitor the texts they read in school and the tasks provided in the study.

The abstract below preceded Markman's full report in *Child Development* and provides clear indication of the specially developed experimental tasks and conditions.

This paper raises the question of how people become aware of their own comprehension failure. It is argued that a partial answer to this question can be derived from recent demonstrations that comprehension involves constructive processing. People might detect certain types of problems in their comprehension as a result of information obtained while engaged in constructive processing. To the extent that children are failing to engage in such processing, they would not have this source of information and consequently would be misled into thinking they comprehend material they in fact do not understand. In two studies, first through third graders were presented with instructions made obviously incomprehensible by deleting information needed to understand how to perform the task. Third graders noticed the inadequacy of the instructions with minimal probing. In contrast, first graders had to be urged to enact the instructions before becoming aware of the problems. When demonstrations of the tasks accompanied the instructions, children more readily indicated that they failed to understand. Since demonstrations and enactments both reduce the necessity for mental processing, these results support the hypothesis that children's initial sensitivity to their own comprehension failures is due to a relative lack of constructive processing.

In contrast to Markman's approach, naturalistic researchers studying the same issue might have installed a video tape recorder in the classroom or visited the classroom frequently as participant-observers to watch for ways in which the children dealt with the information within the classroom context of their usual school day. They might even have made periodic visits to the homes to learn more about how the children made sense of incomplete information in their home environments.

How These Differences
Affect Data Gathering and Data Reporting

While an experimental researcher might attempt to gather data in as naturalistic a setting as possible, and a naturalistic researcher might ask children to engage in planned tasks, the overall stance of the two would be quite different. One's primary focus would likely be on the segment of behavior or learning being examined, while the other's focus would be on understanding that behavior within the interactive framework of the environment in which the behavior occurs.

Ann Haas Dyson, a naturalistic researcher, reported her study, "The Role of Oral Language in Early Writing Processes," in *Research in the Teach-*

ing of English (1983). To study young children's writing, she placed a writing corner in the classroom and, over three months' time, she visited the classroom daily to observe the children's writing behaviors. She spoke with the children and asked questions to understand their reasoning. The abstract that preceded Dyson's journal report clearly indicates her naturalistic bias.

Participant observation was used to examine the role of oral language in early writing. Data collection took place daily over a three-month period in a kindergarten classroom. The researcher set up a writing center in which the children were asked simply to write, according to their own definition of writing. She observed and interacted with the children to gain insight into their perceptions of writing and their reasoning about writing behaviors, focusing particularly on five children selected as case studies. Data consisted of audiotaped recordings of the children's talk at the center, written products, observational notes, and interviews with the children and their parents. Findings included analyses of children's talk while writing and hypotheses regarding each child's knowledge of the relationship between talk and writing. On the basis of these findings, developmental inferences were made regarding how children use speech to make sense of written language: initially talk is used to invest written graphics with meaning; eventually talk is viewed as the substance of written language.

In contrast, some experimental researchers, looking at the same issue, might have been more concerned with holding the writing tasks constant across children and therefore might have attempted to regulate the kind of writing the children did by providing story-starters or specific topics.

Research reports representing different orientations also differ in their view of how learning operates and how distortions that affect the findings reflect the theoretical biases of researchers. The experimental researcher might carefully describe the kinds of behaviors being analyzed, explain the conditions under which those behaviors were isolated (for example, the specific questions or tasks presented to stimulate the particular behavior), and describe how, across children, certain variables that might create differences in the behaviors (such as age, grade, IQ, or achievement level) were held constant or in some other way accounted for. In contrast, the naturalistic researcher might carefully focus on the environment and describe the different people and/or events that might have affected learning in that particular environment (for instance, the student-teacher interaction, the student-classmate interaction, or the physical environment).

In the studies cited above, Markman and Dyson each described their data-gathering procedures. While Markman attempted to be friendly toward the children and help them feel comfortable with her, the classroom setting was clearly not an issue in her study.

> Before the start of the experiment, the experimenter introduced herself to the class and announced that she was attempting to find effective ways to teach children how to play games and perform magic tricks. She emphasized that she needed the students' help in determining the adequacy of her instructions and that students would be asked to suggest improvements in the instructions. Each child was seen individually and administered the two tasks (game and magic trick) in counterbalanced order. Before each task, children were reminded to inform the experimenter if there was anything at all that she failed to state clearly enough or forgot to tell them.

On the other hand, Dyson was quite concerned with her interactions with the children within their class. The comparability of tasks was clearly not an issue in her study.

> I gathered the data for this study daily from October through December, 1980. The data were collected primarily in the morning, between 8:45 and 10:30, during the children's "center" or free-choice period. Data collection proceeded through three general, overlapping phases. Each phase is briefly described in the following sections.
>
> Phase I (Weeks 1–3): Preliminary observation/ initial assessment. During this phase, I observed and interacted with the children as they worked in their centers. My role as participant was that of an interested, nonthreatening adult (see Corsaro, 1981 for a detailed discussion of strategies for field entry in participant observation studies). I adopted what Corsaro (1981, p. 118) refers to as a "reactive" field entry strategy. Rather than directing or monitoring the children's activities, I followed their leads. . . .

How These Differences
Affect Analyses and Reporting

While both experimental and naturalistic researchers might describe events or use statistics to analyze their data, differences can be seen in the ways in which the analyses are developed. Experimentalists design their experiments to observe some predetermined behaviors, as Markman did.

> When a child asked a clearly adequate question (or made a relevant statement), the procedure was terminated. A child was given a separate score for the magic and game conditions which indicated at what point in the procedure he or she asked an appropriate question. The scores ranged from 1 to 11. Scores from 1 to 10 corresponded to the 10 probes in the procedure. An 11 indicated that the child never asked a question.
>
> A child's question was considered adequate if it indicated that the child knew he or she did not understand the instructions (in whole or in part) or that the experimenter had omitted information, etc. . . . .

Analyses would focus on identifying cognitive dimensions of those students who did and those who did not identify the inconsistencies.

Naturalistic researchers most often gather the data first, carefully examine it for patterns, and let their analyses emerge from those patterns. This was Dyson's approach.

> At the end of the eleventh week of observation, I had recorded approximately 36 hours of spontaneous talk, collected approximately 500 written products, made 112 observations of focal children, and written notations on 377 child visits to the writing center.
>
> The analysis procedure was inductive. I began by organizing the data into analytic categories. Since the research question concerned the role of oral language in the writing process, I identified categories of both the writing process in general and the functions accompanying talk in particular. The identification process was one of classifying and reclassifying data under different organizers (see Corsaro, p. 319). I initially based the analysis on the data collected during the first two weeks of the post assessment observational period (phase 2). However, the resulting categories were continually modified and refined during the construction of the case studies.

As in the abstract and procedures sections, the reporting of the analyses is clearly different. Even in cases where the treatments might appear to be similar, each researcher's stance in describing the analyses is likely to be revealing: One would be more holistic and focussed on interactions in the environment, and one would be more concerned with the behavior being studied and how it fits into the bigger behavioral or learning pattern.

How These Differences
Affect the Structure of the Report

Although many researchers combine methodologies and do not appear to emanate distinctly from one of the traditions described above, their theoretical leanings are often revealed in the organizational formats of their research reports. The most widely known research report format grows out of the experimentalist focus and generally includes these sections:

a. theoretical *background*—why the study was undertaken, and how the work relates to previous related studies.

b. the *study* itself—who the *subjects* were and how they were selected, what *materials* were developed and/or selected for use, and what the research *methods* and *procedures* (such as the when and how of data collection) were.

c. the *analyses* and *findings*—how the data were analyzed, most often with reference to the statistical procedures, and the *results* of those analyses.

d. the *conclusions*—what syntheses and generalizations can be made from the results, and a *discussion* of what that means in terms of our understandings of that behavior, and

e. the *implications*—what effect the findings have on research, on teaching, or on the field in general.

The emphasized words frequently serve as section headings of reports with an experimental focus. However, even when the headings are absent or replaced with other terms, the specific kinds of information are almost always given in the order presented above.

Markman's research report is organized in the following manner:

Background (with no heading)
Study I
    Method
        Subjects
        Procedure
        Scoring
    Results and Discussion

Study II
 Method
  Subjects
  Procedure
 Results and Discussion
General Discussion

Unlike this fairly standard experimentalist format, research reports growing out of a naturalistic orientation tend to be more varied in organization. Dyson's paper contains some of the headings listed above, although her study is clearly not experimental. Because the experimental research tradition has a long history in educational (particularly reading) research, and its format is more familiar to many readers than the naturalistic report, some researchers choose the more familiar format to present their nonexperimental work.

Dyson's report is organized in the following manner:

Background
 The functions of oral language
 The development of writing as symbolization
 The processes of early writing
Method
 Site
 Participants
 Data Collection Procedures
Data Analysis
 Categories of Analysis
 Case Studies
Discussion
 Early Writing Processes
 Theoretical Interpretations
Summary

Although Dyson used the headings generally associated with experimentally based research, some language in her subsections suggests that her report is naturalistically based: (1) under *Method*, she used the word *Participants* as opposed to *Subjects*, and (2) under *Data Analysis*, she used the term *Categories of Analysis* as opposed to *Data Analyses* or simply *Analyses*.

Unlike Dyson, other naturalistic researchers prefer to use headings even more clearly representative of their research interests. Gearhart and

Newman's report (1980) of their study, "Learning to Draw a Picture: The Social Context of An Individual Activity," is organized in the following manner:

Background (with no heading)
The Social Organization of Individual Drawing Tasks
    Peer Imitation
    Imitations to the Teacher Across Tasks
    Implications for Learning to Draw
Drawing Tasks as Teacher-Child Tutorials
    Were the Children Planful?
    Teacher Planfulness
    Negotiating the Finish
    Ownership
    The Finish Discussion
    Implications for Learning to Draw
Conclusion

Because entering and describing the child's world is the naturalistic researchers' method of understanding behavior and learning, they prefer to describe the *context* or *environment* as a whole with special attention to specific aspects of the environment that interact during learning and therefore affect learning. These reports also generally describe the manner in which the *interactions, communications,* or *negotiations* were *observed,* what kind of *data* were collected (for example, field notes, audio or video tapes, or writing samples), what *patterns* were found in the data, and how they were *categorized* and *analyzed.* These analyses are frequently used to reflect on the kinds of interactions that do or could affect learning. Although *background* information is often provided to place the study within a theoretical context of inquiry, and *summaries* and *generalizations* presented as well, no typical sequence or organizational system is used. Because of this, it is important for readers to know what underlying concepts framed the study; only then can they know what information to look for, whatever the order within the text of the report. Some of these concepts have been emphasized above, and report readers should expect to find the issues around them reported, whether or not the words themselves appear in the report.

How to Read
Research Reports Flexibly

The research report reader has a specific purpose for reading the report—frequently because it deals with a topic the reader wants to know more about. A first reading is rarely done straight through, from beginning to end. Many readers first get a general notion of what the report is about and then decide whether or not to read it more carefully. This first quick reading sets expectations about the format and topic of the report that assist the reader in getting more information during a second, more careful reading.

Most readers begin with a reading of the abstract to get an overview of the study and its findings. When no abstract is present, or after the abstract has been completed, many readers turn to the introductory section that describes the goals of the study and places it into a larger theoretical framework. From there, readers generally turn to the discussion or conclusion section to get a general impression of the findings and their implications. While these sections are often easy to spot because of the section headings in the more experimentally based articles, they are usually included somewhere in naturalistically based reports, as well. Even when the report begins with a series of quotes from children in the study (this is frequently done to set the tone for a naturalistic, child-oriented focus), the theoretical background and questions often follow. Findings may be scattered throughout the narrative of the study, but they are often summarized toward the end of the paper. Occasionally, they are presented or foreshadowed in the opening.

From this first brief look at a research report, the reader can generally decide whether the study will be personally informative, be it for supervisory decisions, teaching techniques, or an academic critique. A closer reading can follow.

The next few chapters will present several specific methodologies, outlining their underlying assumptions and providing examples of actual reports. The reports have been selected to illustrate the content and special language generally included in reports of each sort. The information presented will usually fall within the organizational frameworks described in this chapter.

REFERENCES

Dyson, A. H. (1983). The role of oral language in early writing processes. *Research in the Teaching of English, 17*(1), 1–30.

Gearhart, M., & Newman, D. (1980). Learning to draw a picture: The social context of an individual activity. *Discourse Processes, 3*(2), 169–184.

Markman, E. (1977). Realizing that you don't understand: A preliminary investigation. *Child Development, 48,* 986–992.

Chapter 3

Correlational Research in Reading and Writing

The purpose of reading and writing research is to determine relationships between variables (such as amount of instruction, level of reading ability, or type of practice in writing) and outcomes or events (such as reading achievement, oral reading accuracy, or richness of written work).

In some situations, we want to know what causes something we have observed. One efficient method of doing this is to systematically manipulate parts of the situation, under very carefully controlled conditions, and see what the effects are. Such manipulations involve selecting different values for the variables, such as high reading ability versus low reading ability, or writing in journals versus structured composition practice. The effects on the situation can then be attributed to the changes in the variables.

If things worked out neatly, we would not need other methods of doing research; we could rely strictly on this technique. Unfortunately, the world is not always amenable to our needs or desires to manipulate what we want to. When researchers cannot manipulate situations, they often turn to correlational techniques to describe relationships among variables.

In this chapter, we will discuss those correlational techniques used when researchers encounter problems that cannot be investigated by carefully controlled manipulations and observations. Three general situations require the use of these correlational techniques:

1. When the situation is difficult (or impossible) to control or manipulate;
2. When dealing with tests to see whether they are reliable or valid;
3. When a large number of measurements are made in the same situation—to determine the nature of relationships that exist among those measurements.

(Related to this last point, another use for correlations is found in multi-variate analyses, in which there are many independent or dependent variables. This additional use is discussed in chapter 8 on multiple regressions and multivariate analyses.)

Before we look at examples of how correlations are used in reading and language research, we need to see what a correlation means and represents.

WHAT DOES CORRELATION MEAN?

Correlation is a term applied to a measure of the relationship between two variables. For example, we might know a student's score on a reading readiness test and want to know how well we could predict future reading achievement. The correlation between readiness scores and reading achievement tells how reading achievement changes as readiness scores change.

Correlations are expressed as numbers between -1.0 and $+1.0$. A correlation of $+1.0$ means that one variable can be predicted *without error* from values of the other. The plus ($+$) sign means that the variables are positively related—as one goes up (or down), so does the other. Figure 3–

Figure 3–1
Graph of positive correlation (real value: $r = +0.722$)

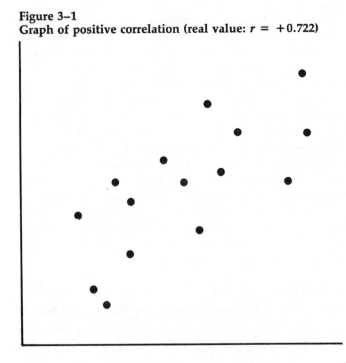

1 is a graph of a correlation that is +0.722. Note that, in general, as the values increase on either dimension, they also increase on the other.

A minus (−) sign means that the variables are negatively or reciprocally related—when one goes up, the other goes down. For example, the correlation between number of word recognition errors and comprehension scores is negative: The greater the number of errors, the lower the comprehension score. Such a correlation is illustrated in Figure 3–2, where the value of the correlation is −0.606.

The further from +1.0 or −1.0 a correlation is, the less able we are to make predictions. So, when two variables have a correlation of 0.0, predictions can be made with a success level only equal to guessing. Figure 3–3 is a graph of a correlation equal to −0.023. It can be seen that there is no precise way to predict scores along one dimension from a score on the other.

In order to determine how predictable one measure is from another, the correlation value is squared. Again, the closer the squared value is to 1.0, the more precise the predictions. Some illustrations will help: Squaring a correlation of 0.2 yields a value of 0.04, while a correlation of 0.7 yields a squared value of 0.49. Thus, even though 0.7 is 2½ times greater than 0.2, the predictions will be over 10 times more precise.

Figure 3–2
Graph of negative correlation (real value: $r = -0.606$)

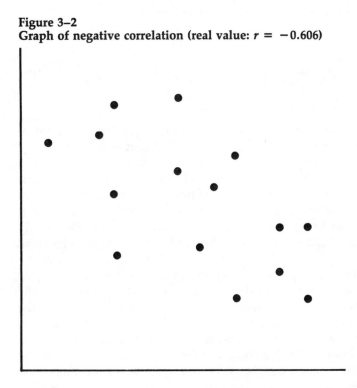

Figure 3–3
Correlation graph for $r = 0$ (actual value: $r = -0.023$)

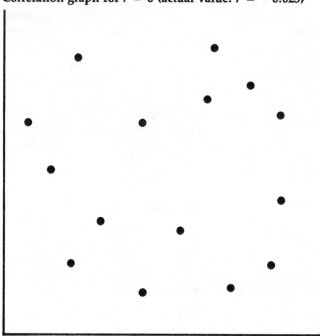

Tests of Significance
for Correlations

As with other statistical tests, once a correlation is calculated, it should be subjected to a test of significance. For a correlation that is calculated on a single sample, a probability is reported. For example, $r = 0.62$, $p < 0.05$ means that, given the number of observations, a correlation of this magnitude would have occurred by chance fewer than five out of one hundredtimes. That is, the correlation value can be assumed with more than 95 percent confidence to be different from 0.0. Critical values can be obtained by referring to tables of these values. One such table is given in appendix B.

At other times, we might ask the question: Is one correlation significantly different from another? In other words, the question is whether the relationship between one set of variables is significantly different from the relationship for another set. In this case, t- or Z-tests are often used to provide the answer. This is not a procedure you will encounter often, but the information obtained in this way can be very effective for making instructional decisions. An example of the use of these tests is illustrated later in this chapter.

Attenuation of Correlation

When we want to interpret correlations, we must be very careful about generalizing the conclusions. A major component of correlation is the amount of variance in the samples. If there is little variance, it is unlikely that there will be a significant correlation, that is, a correlation different from 0.0. Accurate comparison of correlations is limited to samples that have similar variances. For example, we may find a high correlation between test scores and reading achievement for a sample of students from the first to sixth grades. However, if we are trying to predict reading achievement of students in a single grade, the correlation is said to be *attenuated*. Namely, the correlation is smaller than it is for a wider range of grade levels, because the variance is greater over a wider range. Therefore, we might not be able to predict success in reading from the test scores as well as we could overall. Further discussion of attenuation is given in Edwards (1961) or Cronbach (1949).

Correlation and Causation

At this point, we must note emphatically: A correlation, even a high one, does not reveal anything definite about whether one variable *causes* the other. (Although, if one variable did operate by itself consistently and *did* cause another, the correlation should be $+1.0$ or -1.0).

We can see how this is true when we look at a real situation. There is a relatively high correlation between letter-name knowledge and reading achievement in first grade. However, it is difficult to see how knowing the names of letters produces reading achievement. We must determine whether there is some other variable that causes both letter-name knowledge and reading achievement to be high.

WHERE TO LOOK

The material unique to correlational studies is found in three places in a research report. The first place is the Introduction. Sometimes what is intended is discussed; for example, if the authors describe a situation in which they are validating a test, you should be alert for correlations in later sections of the report. Don't be surprised, however, if there are no hard clues about correlations in the Introduction.

The second place to look for clues that the study is correlational is in the Results section. Here the writer should explain the statistical procedures in detail. You should know what was done, as well as what the actual statistical results were.

Finally, there should be some differences in the sorts of conclusions reached in the Discussion section. As we will see, this involves avoiding statements of causality on the basis of correlational data.

Questions to Ask
about Correlational Studies

As with other types of studies, there are certain questions that should be asked to guide the evaluation of correlational studies.

1. What is the purpose of the study?
    a) to study variables that are hard to manipulate?
    b) to investigate the reliability of a test or other instrument?
    c) to determine the relationships among several dependent variables?
2. Was the use of correlation appropriate? (State why.)
3. What were the measures used (unless the study was to investigate reliability)? (Name them.)
4. Was the correlation value statistically significant? (State the value and the probability.)
5. How well can predictions be made with the obtained value? (Give the numerical figure.)
6. Are the generalizations, implications, or conclusions kept within the limits of the study and the statistics used? (Indicate how.)

Types of Correlations

Different types of statistical procedures are used in different situations to arrive at a correlation coefficient. The type of correlational procedure depends on two characteristics: (1) the type of data collected, and (2) the *general* type of relationship between the variables (linear or nonlinear). While the interpretation is similar for all correlations, it is important to know that the use of these different types conveys different information to a reader of research articles.

Pearson Product-Moment (r)

The most commonly used correlation coefficient is called the Pearson product-moment correlation, represented by the symbol "r," as $r = 0.84$. Pearson product-moment correlations assume the relationship between the two variables can best be described by a straight line. The data need to be continuous, not categorical (that is, like scores on a test instead of for a class). Technically, continuous data can assume any value, unrestricted by category limits. In practice, however, as long as the number of categories exceeds about 15–20, categorical data may be treated as if they were continuous.

Spearman Rho (ρ)

When the data to be correlated are available only in ranks, the Spearman Rho correlation is used. (Ranks reflect *only* that one score is greater or less than another, not the differences in magnitude between the scores.) The only difference between the Spearman Rho and the Pearson product-moment correlations is the nature of the data. Although different tests of significance are used, both correlations are interpreted similarly.

The following example of the use of Spearman's ρ is taken from a report of two studies by Ryan, McNamara, and Kenney (1977), "Linguistic awareness and reading performance among beginning readers."

What is the purpose of the study?

The research report contains a section called *Purpose* instead of a more typical *Introduction*. The *Purpose* section reads:

> Vygotsky (1934/1962) and Mattingly (1972) proposed that the contrast between the ease, universality, and naturalness of oral language learning and the apparent difficulty of learning to read can be explained by regarding reading as a deliberately learned language-based skill, depending upon the speaker's awareness of primary linguistic activity. The present study investigates the relationships between various aspects of linguistic awareness and early reading ability.

Was the use of correlation appropriate?

As noted earlier, a reader can often predict what sort of analysis will be used from the nature of the experimental questions. In this case, the word "relationships" is a clue to look for correlations later in the paper. Specifically, notice that the writers are not looking for differences but trying to discover relationships.

> *What were the measures used?*
> *Was the correlation statistically significant?*
> *How well can predictions be made with the obtained correlation value?*

In another section titled *Analysis* (instead of the more common *Results*), the authors write:

> Also, the Sentence Comparison Task exhibited a similar but nonsignificant trend. Significant Spearman

correlation coefficients were obtained among three of the four oral tasks: Word Discrimination with Sentence Comparison, $r = .65$, $p < .01$; Word Discrimination with Multigrammatical Function Word, $r = .65$, $p < .01$; and Sentence Comparison with Multigrammatical Function Word, $r = .62$, $p < .01$.

Note that the researchers analyzed the rank orders, rather than the actual scores. (In this study, the researchers did test for differences between groups with t-tests, but the correlations are the focus of our present discussion.) However, the correlations are still high and significantly different from 0.0.

Are the generalizations, implications, or conclusions kept within the limits of the study and the statistics used?

The place to look for clues to interpreting a research report that uses correlations is in the *Discussion* or *Conclusion* section. In their report, Ryan, McNamara, and Kenney (1977) write:

Performance on all linguistic awareness tasks except ·Word Tapping reflected a substantial advantage of better readers over poorer readers. The results for first and second graders are quite similar to those for the older remedial readers. The failure of the Word Tapping Task to relate to reading level or the other measures is discrepant with earlier findings with younger children. Further research is required to determine whether the task is not sensitive to individual differences among beginning readers or whether procedural changes can make it more effective. The causal relationship among measures of linguistic awareness and development of reading skills remains to be explored via training studies.

Note that the researchers are not claiming that the variables *cause* one another. They are suggesting that, since the correlations are high, attempts should be made to find out whether the variables are causally related.

Other Correlations

A substantial number of other correlations may be encountered infrequently in reading research. They are designed to be used when researchers come upon situations that make the use of more familiar procedures inappropriate.

If the data to be analyzed have a nonlinear relationship, a procedure is used that yields a correlation coefficient known as *Eta* (η). Figure 3–4 shows a graph of a nonlinear relationship between two variables. Once again, this is interpreted similarly to other correlations, but it is calculated and tested for significance by different procedures. As a reader, though, you should be aware of the basic nature of the relationship between the two variables.

When data are collected in a dichotomous fashion (for instance, yes or no) and correlations are to be calculated, several methods can be used, depending on the assumptions underlying the variables. Among these are *point biserial, phi coefficient, tetrachoric,* and the *biserial coefficient.* A thorough discussion of these is found in Edwards (1961).

CORRELATION AND TESTING

Reliability

The concept of *reliability* involves asking whether a test will give the same results when administered on more than one occasion. There are, in general, three types of reliability:

Figure 3–4
Graph of nonlinear relationship

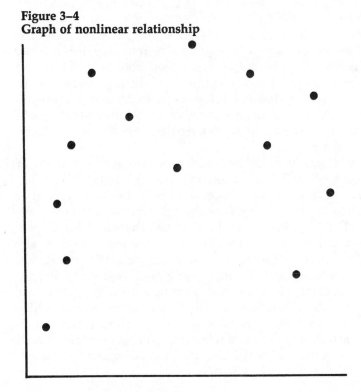

1. test-retest reliability;
2. split-half reliability; and
3. alternate forms reliability.

Briefly, *test-retest* reliability asks whether the test gives the same score over time. While the techniques for calculating reliability are not the same as those for correlations, it is convenient to conceptualize reliability as if it were a correlation. Thus, test-retest reliability can be thought of as the correlation between the scores on two administrations of the same test.

Split-half reliability measures whether or not different portions of the same test yield similar scores. In this case, reliability can be thought of as a correlation between the scores on different portions of the test (for instance, first half versus second half, or odd items versus even items). One caution should be noted: Split-half reliability is sensitive to the length of a test—the longer the test, the higher the reliability. Reliability also depends on which halves of the text are selected. For example, odds versus evens will give different estimates from first half versus second half. For this reason, reliability in these cases is best estimated by using a statistic known as Cronbach's Alpha. (For a discussion of this topic, see Thorndike and Hagen 1977, 73–84.)

Finally, if more than one form of a test exists, *alternate forms* reliability measures the degree to which scores from those different forms are equivalent. Here, the reliability can be thought of as the correlation between the scores on the two forms of the test.

The numbers used to express reliability are interpreted like correlations, although they are calculated in slightly different ways from other correlations. Reliability is expressed as a number from 0.0 to 1.0. The interpretation is similar to that for correlations. That is, for values close to 1.0, the reliability is nearly perfect; for values close to 0.0, the reliability is nil. Note, however, that there are no negative reliabilities—that would mean that a student who scored high on a first administration would be likely to score low on a second.

Most often reliability is calculated either by using one of a set of formulas developed by Kuder-Richardson or by using Cronbach's Alpha. The Kuder-Richardson formulas are abbreviated by initials and a number denoting a specific formula to be used for the appropriate conditions, for example K-R 20 or K-R 21. These formulas compare the variability in performance on each test item with the variability of the entire test. If performance on the individual items is very different from the overall test performance, then the test has low reliability. If performance on the individual items is consistent and in general agreement with the overall test results, then the test has high reliability. The Kuder-Richardson formulas provide an index of this type of consistency. (If you are interested in pursuing more of the technical details of reliability, you may want to consult some of the readings at the end of the chapter. A good treatment is given in Thorndike and Hagen [1977, 56–107].)

The following study was conducted by George Hanna.

What is the purpose of the study?
Was the use of correlation appropriate?

In this example, the researcher applies the concepts of reliability and corrections for attenuation to the measurement of passage dependence. Passage dependence is an attribute of comprehension questions. Questions that can be answered only by reading the text are called passage *dependent;* those that can be answered without reading are passage *independent.* Hanna (1979) compared several measures of context dependence, a more general case of passage dependence.

What were the measures used?

The section cited is from *Procedures:*

> For each Part II item in each form, the Pyrczak *I* was computed. For the 30 items in each form, the 10 having the best *I*'s and the 10 having the worst *I*'s were identified. In each form, CP subscores were then obtained from these two subgroups of items. For each set of 10 CP items, the mean, standard deviation, and Kuder-Richardson Formula 20 reliability coefficient was then computed. For each form, the correlation between subscores obtained from the CP items having the best and the worst *I*'s was next computed. Finally, this correlation coefficient for each form was corrected for attenuation.
> These procedures were then repeated for the Tuinman and Hanna-Oaster indices.

The following is taken from a combined *Findings and Discussion:*

> Turning now to the major findings, [Table 3–1] shows for each index and each form the mean, standard deviation, and K-R 20 estimate of internal consistency for the group of 10 best and 10 worst items as well as the original and corrected correlation between these two sets of scores. The key findings for each index is the extent to which the scores of the group of 10 best and 10 worst items are intercorrelated after correction for attenuation.
> The correct correlation for each form between scores of the 10 reading comprehension items having the best Pyrczak indices and the 10 worst Pyrczak

Table 3–1
Descriptive and correlational findings from reading comprehension test

Index	Item Group	Form 3A (n = 131)					Form 3B (n = 125)				
					Intercorrelation					Intercorrelation	
		$\bar{X}$	SD	K-R 20	Raw	Corrected	$\bar{X}$	SD	K-R 20	Raw	Corrected
Pyrczak	10 Best	3.6	1.9	.46	.58	1.14	3.2	2.2	.62	.63	1.06
	10 Worst	4.9	2.2	.58			4.8	2.2	.57		
Tuinman	10 Best	6.0	2.4	.68	.46	.90	4.7	2.4	.65	.30	.56
	10 Worst	3.3	1.5	.38			2.6	1.7	.42		
Hanna-Oaster	10 Best	6.2	2.4	.68	.49	.97	5.2	2.6	.73	.28	.47
	10 Worst	3.1	1.6	.38			2.3	1.8	.49		

Source: Hanna 1979, 333. Used with permission of the National Reading Conference.

indices is greater than 1.00. This means that with the test content used in the sample studied the attribute measured by items having the best Pyrczak indices was the identical attribute, or at the very least was perfectly correlated with the attribute, measured by items having the worst Pyrczak indices; the subscores intercorrelated as highly as their respective reliabilities would allow. In this situation, CD [context dependence] as defined by the Pyrczak index seems to be a topic involving meaningless labeling of items.

The corrected correlations between scores from the 10 items with the best and worst Tuinman indices are .90 and .56 for the two forms. The extent to which these are less than 1.00 indicates that the attribute measured by items with good Tuinman indices is somewhat independent from the attribute measured by items with poor Tuinman indices. . . . While both Tuinman and Hanna-Oaster indices excelled the Pyrczak index, no consistent difference between the former two indices emerged.

Was the correlation value statistically significant?
How well can predictions be made with the obtained value?

Note several items as you read this example. First, correction for attenuation is necessary, since the researcher used only the 10 best and worst items. The correction *statistically* estimates what the correlation would have been had all the items been used. The assumptions of the statistical test were not quite met. The researchers were trying to correct statistically for the problems generated by not having met the assumptions. What is important here is that the corrected correlation exceeds 1.00. This happens in unusual cases and should be taken to mean that the value is 1.00 or very close to it. Because the statistics are estimations, they are sometimes in error.

A second point is the use of the K-R 20 reliability estimates. These values are not as high as we might expect, because they are based on only 10 items. In general, the more items (or the longer the test), the more reliable it will be.

Are the generalizations, implications, or conclusions kept within
the limits of the study and the statistics used?

Finally, not every piece of research is going to have direct application to classroom practice. In this case, the author is investigating ways of making tests more sensitive to the material they are to evaluate. Be aware that not all tests are carefully matched to the specific passages (contexts) they are to assess.

Validity

A second use of correlation in testing is to establish the validity of a test—to determine if the test measures what it was designed to measure. (A more thorough discussion of different types of validity is given in Campbell and Stanley [1963] and Thorndike and Hagen [1977].) To establish validity, test developers use a generally accepted method of measurement and report the correlation of scores obtained in that manner with the scores obtained by the new method. This is known as *concurrent validity*. High correlations indicate high validity. If the old measures were valid, so are the new ones.

The following example is taken from a study by Cunningham and Cunningham (1978) in which they were trying to establish the validity of a limited-cloze procedure.

What is the purpose of the study?
Was the use of correlation appropriate?
What were the measures used?

In Study I, a limited-cloze test constructed from a Passage B was compared with a regular cloze test constructed from Passage B as to which test's scores would better predict scores of a regular cloze test constructed from a Passage A. In Study II, the Passage B/limited-cloze test was compared with the Passage B/regular cloze test as to which test's scores would better predict scores of a reading comprehension test which used comprehension questions.

Study I

Seventh-grade subjects from southeastern Ohio were randomly assigned to two groups; complete data were obtained from 163 of these subjects. Group 1 (N = 84) was administered a regular 20% cloze test constructed from Passage A, followed, the next day, by a regular 20% cloze test constructed from Passage B. Group 2 (N = 79) was administered the regular cloze test constructed from Passage A, followed, the next day, by a limited-cloze test constructed from Passage B. Using the Passage A/regular cloze test as the criterion a concurrent validity coefficient was computed for each test format of Passage B by correlating Passage A test scores with Passage B test scores for each group.

The correlation between Passage A/regular cloze scores and Passage B/regular cloze scores was .584 (*p*

< .001) with the KR 21 reliability of Passage B/regular cloze being .64. The correlation between Passage A/regular cloze and Passage B/limited-cloze scores was .558 ($p < .001$) with the KR 21 reliability of Passage B/limited-cloze being .85.

This evidence supports the validity of using a limited-cloze test constructed from a passage as a substitute for a regular cloze test constructed from that passage. Moreover, limited-cloze appears at least as reliable, if not more so, than the regular cloze.

Study II

Fifth-grade subjects from Piedmont, North Carolina were also randomly assigned to two groups; complete data were obtained from 203 of these subjects. Group 1 (N = 98) was administered the Passage B/regular cloze test while Group 2 was administered the Passage B/limited-cloze test. A week later, both groups were administered the reading comprehension subtest of the *Iowa Tests of Basic Skills* (1971).

The correlation between reading comprehension subtest scores and Passage B/regular cloze scores was .593 ($p < .001$) with a KR 21 reliability of .70 for the cloze test. The correlation between reading comprehension subtest scores and Passage B/limited-cloze scores was .733 (p < .001) with a KR 21 reliability of .90 for the limited-cloze test. The difference between the validity coefficients was not significant (Z = 1.77, $p < .08$).

This evidence further supports the validity of the limited-cloze as a substitute for the regular cloze, and, taken with the results of Study I, suggests that the limited-cloze may be more reliable than regular cloze.

Was the correlation value statistically significant?
How well can predictions be made with the obtained value?
Are the generalizations, implications, or conclusions kept within the limits of the study and the statistics used?

The authors have introduced us to the concept of *concurrent validity*. This simply means that if the generally accepted measure is valid, the new measure is also valid to the extent that it correlates with the old. In this case, the concurrent validity scores are reasonable though not exceptionally high.

For the measures of reliability, the authors found that their new procedure (limited cloze) was somewhat more reliable than the traditional cloze. This means that scores from the limited cloze are probably more stable than those from standard cloze. Such stability would be desirable for making instructional decisions.

Finally, the authors tested the difference between the validity coefficients. They had already found out that they were both different from 0.0. Now they wanted to know whether they were different from each other. They found that they were not, although the difference between validity coefficients was fairly large, The conclusion is simply that neither of the procedures is *more* valid than the other—that is, neither can predict comprehension better than the other.

CORRELATIONS AND MULTIPLE MEASURES

In the opening chapters, we saw the importance of the notion of ecological validity (see chapter 1). One solution to making certain that experiments are valid is to take a large number of measures in any situation. With some data collection techniques, it is possible to collect more data than we can analyze. Computers have allowed us the luxury of collecting such large amounts of data and have made it possible to analyze it all.

However, when we take multiple measures, we run the risk of measuring the same thing with two or more similar measures. To guard against interpreting this inappropriately, we usually want to look at the *intercorrelations* between the various measures. This can tell us whether or not we are measuring the same phenomena in the same way. For example, if we have two measures that correlate highly, we do not need both. If they are uncorrelated ($r = 0.0$), different conclusions might be based on the interpretation of each.

The following example is taken from Tierney, Bridge, and Cera (1978–79), *Results and Discussion*.

> *What is the purpose of the study?*
> *Was the use of correlation appropriate?*

> Intercorrelational analysis and several repeated measures analyses of variance provided further clarification. Specifically, intercorrelational analyses afforded an examination of the nature of the relationship between the various scores across subjects. (1978–79, 549)

> *What were the measures used?*
> *Was the correlation value significant?*

Table 3–2 is also from the Tierney, Bridge, and Cera report. A great deal of information is packed into this table. In fact, three sets of correlations

Table 3–2

Intercorrelations among selected indexes for all children[a] and for good and poor readers[b]

		1	2	3	4	5	6	7	8	9	10
Free	1 Total Expl.		.70	−.26	.98	.77	−.17	.32	.33	−.20	.09
	2 Total Infer.	.63 .52		.34	.64	.72	−.01	.25	.09	−.05	.18
	3 Infer./Expl.	−.08 −.18	.67 .60		−.31	−.03	.11	−.05	−.21	.08	.15
	4 Semantic	.95 .98	.50 .49	−.19 −.20		.64	−.19	.27	.29	−.22	.11
	5 Logical	.69 .31	.74 .21	.34 .05	.48 .11		−.17	.36	.36	−.06	−.11
Probed	6 Total Expl.	−.46 .18	−.07 −.02	.41 −.10	−.47 .03	−.28 .73		.03	−.39	.98	.48
	7 Total Infer.	.09 .22	.12 .09	.09 −.00	.01 .15	.20 .40	−.18 .55		.46	.04	−.06
	8 Infer./Expl.	.09 .12	−.12 −.03	−.25 −.11	.02 .15	.20 −.07	−.49 −.13	.40 .65		−.36	−.28
	9 Semantic	−.46 .13	−.07 −.10	.41 −.17	−.48 −.01	−.22 .70	.99 .98	−.15 .52	−.45 −.12		.30
	10 Logical	−.26 .20	−.04 .37	.25 .37	−.23 .20	−.41 −.00	.60 −.11	−.23 .03	−.50 .01	.46 −.31	

[a]Upper right side of matrix lists intercorrelations for all children.
[b]Lower left side of matrix lists within each matrix cell intercorrelations for good readers and poor readers. The intercorrelation for good readers is listed over the intercorrelation for poor readers.
Source: Tierney, Bridge, and Cera 1978–79, 550. Reprinted with permission of the author and the International Reading Association.

are represented. One set is for all of the children studied, another is for the poor readers, and the last is for the good readers. What is missing in the table is the level of significance for the entries. For correlations, it is easy to find out what those levels should be.

First, we need to know the number of students in each group. By referring to the *Method* section, we can find out what the numbers were. Tierney, Bridge, and Cera used 18 good readers and 18 poor readers. That means that there are 16 degrees of freedom (df) associated with each of the correlations in the lower left of the table and 34 df for each of the entries in the upper right. *Degrees of freedom* are an index of the sensitivity of the statistic being used. For correlations, df are based on the number of subjects and the number of observations. As the df increases, so does the sensitivity of the statistic.

We then need to find a table of significant values for Pearson product correlations. (We can generally assume correlations are Pearson product-moment values, unless it is otherwise specified.) Such a table is included in appendix B. By entering it with 16 df, we find that, to be significantly different from 0.0, a correlation must be 0.468; for 34 df, the value is 0.325. In both cases, we have chosen $p < 0.05$. Other values for p can be selected. We can use the same value for negative correlations.

> *How well can predictions be made with the obtained value?*
> *Are the generalizations, implications, or conclusions kept within*
> *the limits of the study and the statistics used?*

Now the interpretation is a matter of looking at the correlations in the matrix. Correlations above the significant value mean that the information in both indices is similar. As a rule of thumb, we can describe correlations as high (above approximately 0.60), medium (from approximately 0.4 to 0.6), and low (below 0.4). This is a different judgement from whether a correlation is significant or not. Correlations below the significant values mean that we cannot tell one score by knowing the other. Therefore, nonsignificant correlations mean that we can obtain different information from the two measures. As an example, the information from variable 1 (total explicit items recalled) has a correlation of $r = 0.98$ with variable 4 (semantic information). Explanations based on one are likely to be similar to those based on the other. However, the low correlation of variable 1 with variable 10 (logical information) indicates that explanations will be different for these two variables.

CORRELATION
AND NONMANIPULABLE VARIABLES

The last situation in which you are likely to find correlations is when the variables of interest are difficult to manipulate, either for ethical or other reasons. As mentioned in chapter 1, we would not be willing to perform an experiment in which we might produce serious educational deficits in some students. At other times, we have to conduct our studies in situations that we cannot change. To study the effects of class size on reading achievement, ideally, we would alter the number of students in a class over the course of study.

A less disruptive design for such a study could incorporate correlational techniques. In short, classrooms of any size could be used as they were found. Correlations would show the type of relationship that existed between the different numbers of students in a class and their reading achievement scores. Note, however, that this approach entails other problems. For instance, since it is not easy to find a wide range of class sizes, the correlations are not necessarily reflective of the true relationship between class size and achievement.

The following example is taken from a study investigating word recognition in second-grade students (McCormick and Samuels 1979).

What is the purpose of the study?
Was the use of correlation appropriate?

In this study, the authors were interested in the relationship between speed of word recognition, accuracy of word recognition, and oral and silent reading comprehension.

What were the measures used?
Was the correlation value statistically significant?

In the *Results* section, they write:

[Table 3–3] shows the Pearson correlation coefficients among accuracy, latency of words accurately recognized, and comprehension. The correlations indicate that latency and accuracy were significantly correlated with each other on both first-grade and second-grade words. The absolute value of the correlation was .88 for both grade levels, significant beyond the .001 level. Accuracy and latency were each significantly correlated with the total comprehension score on both first-

Table 3–3
Correlation coefficients

Variables	First Grade Words			Second Grade Words		
	N	Pearson *r*	Sig. Level	*N*	Pearson *r*	Sig. Level
Latency with Accuracy	26	−.88	.001	24	−.88	.001
Latency with Total Comprehension	26	−.54	.002	24	−.56	.001
Accuracy with Total Comprehension	26	.49	.006	24	.70	.001
Silent Comprehension with Oral Comprehension	26	.52	.003	24	.64	.001

Latency: average latency between onset of word and correct recognition
Accuracy: Proportion of word list accurately recognized
Total Comprehension: total oral and silent comprehension scores on Gray Oral and SRA stories
Source: McCormick and Samuels 1979, 112. Used with permission of the National Reading Conference.

and second-grade words. The absolute values of the correlations ranged from .49 to .70 and all were significant beyond the .006 level. In summary, high accuracy and rapid word recognition were associated with high comprehension. (1979, 111–12)

As you read the excerpt from this study, think about the rationale for using correlations. It is difficult to manipulate comprehension or accuracy of word recognition. Instead, the researchers measured them and looked at the relationships. Remember, their conclusions should not indicate that they have found causal relationships; rather, they have found two variables (in each case) that can be predicted from each other.

How well can predictions be made with the obtained value?

It is also important to note how well each of the variables can be predicted. The accuracy of prediction ranges from 0.24 to 0.77. Latency and accuracy can be predicted from each other much more precisely than the other variables.

Finally, notice that some of the correlations in Table 3–3 are negative, which means the variables are inversely related—as one goes up, the other goes down. Thus, the shorter the latency, the higher the accuracy or comprehension score. Long latencies are associated with poor accuracy or low comprehension scores.

IN SUMMARY

Correlational research has several major uses in studying reading and writing:

1. Determining relations among variables when they are hard or impossible to manipulate.
2. Determining the reliability of testing instruments.
3. Determining the interrelationships among a number of dependent variables in a given situation.

The major advantage of correlational approaches is that they do not require manipulations of the situations to discover relations between variables. The disadvantage of using correlational methods is that the researcher cannot make statements about causal links between the variables under study. However, since high correlation should suggest other causal links, this may not always be a major problem.

As a reader, you should be aware of the purpose and assumptions underlying the use of correlations. You should also make certain that the appropriate tests of significance were performed. Finally, you should make certain that the interpretation does not exceed the limits of this sort of study. No inference of causation should be based solely on the presence or absence of a significant correlation.

REFERENCES

Campbell, D., & Stanley, J. (1963). *Experimental and quasi-experimental designs for research.* Chicago: Rand McNally.

Cronbach, L. (1949). *Essentials of psychological testing.* New York: Harper.

Cunningham, J., & Cunningham, P. (1978). Validating a limited-cloze procedure. *Journal of Reading Behavior, 10,* 211–213.

Edwards, A. (1961). *Statistical methods for the behavioral sciences.* New York: Holt, Rinehart and Winston.

Hanna, G. (1979). An improved design for examining the importance of context dependence. *Journal of Reading Behavior, 11,* 329–337.

McCormick, C., & Samuels, S. J. (1979). Word recognition by second graders: The unit of perception and interrelationships among accuracy, latency, and comprehension. *Journal of Reading Behavior, 11,* 107–118.

Ryan, E. B., McNamara, S., & Kenney, M. (1977). Linguistic awareness and reading performance among beginning readers. *Journal of Reading Behavior, 11,* 399–400.

Thorndike, R., & Hagen, E. (1977). *Measurement and evaluation in psychology and education.* New York: John Wiley and Sons.

Tierney, R., Bridge, C., & Cera, M. (1978–79). The discourse processing operations of children. *Reading Research Quarterly, 14,* 539–573.

ADDITIONAL EXAMPLES
OF CORRELATIONAL STUDIES

Freedman, S. (1981). Influences on evaluators of expository essays: Beyond the text. *Research in the teaching of English, 15,* 245–255.

Langer, J. (1984). The effects of available information on responses to school writing tasks. *Research in the Teaching of English, 18,* 27–44.

Leu, D., Jr. (1982). Differences between oral and written discourse and the acquisition of reading proficiency. *Journal of Reading Behavior, 14,* 111–125.

Morr, M., & Kamil, M. (1981). Single word decoding and comprehension: A constructive replication. *Journal of Reading Behavior, 13,* 81–86.

Oney, B., & Toldman, S. (1984). Decoding and comprehension skills in Turkish and English: Effects of the regularity of grapheme-phoneme correspondences. *Journal of Educational Psychology, 76,* 557–568.

Stanovich, K., Cunningham, A., & West, R. (1981). A longitudinal study of the development of automatic recognition skills in first graders. *Journal of Reading Behavior, 13,* 57–74.

Tunmer, W., & Fletcher, C. (1981). The relationship between conceptual tempo, phonological awareness, and word recognition in beginning readers. *Journal of Reading Behavior, 13,* 173–185.

ADDITIONAL READING
ABOUT CORRELATIONS

Blalock, H. (1960). *Social Statistics*. New York: McGraw-Hill.

Cook, L., & Campbell, D. (1979). *Quasi-experimental design and analysis for field settings*. Chicago: Rand-McNally.

Hays, W. L. (1973). *Statistics for the social sciences*. New York: Holt.

Shavelson, R. (1981). *Statistical reasoning for the behavioral sceinces*. Boston: Allyn and Bacon.

Siegel, S. (1956). *Nonparametric statistics for the behavioral sciences*. New York: McGraw-Hill.

Chapter 4

Descriptive Research

Descriptive research describes or delineates the characteristics or properties of groups, events, or phenomena. This chapter will define the nature of descriptive research and explore the methods used to collect descriptive research data. It will also examine those characteristics of descriptive research that distinguish it from other research approaches, such as ethnographies or experimental studies. Finally, specific questions that critical readers can use to increase their understanding of descriptive studies are provided, and the use of these questions is demonstrated.

The descriptive research approach, actually a diverse collection of techniques, attempts to specify the way things are *with no experimental manipulation*. Descriptive techniques are used to measure: (1) the existence and distribution of various naturally occurring behaviors or characteristics; (2) the frequencies of occurrence of naturally occurring events; and (3) the relationships and magnitudes of relationship that might exist between the behaviors, characteristics, and events of interest.

To carry out such research, the investigator must have explicit expectations as to which behaviors or characteristics are important and how these behaviors and characteristics are best measured. The investigator scrupulously tries to avoid altering or manipulating the nature of the environment to be described. Particular care must be exercised to prevent the act of data collection itself from altering the phenomena being studied.

In reading and writing research, these descriptive techniques are useful for answering many questions. For example, descriptive research studies would probably be conducted if the investigator wanted to find out the book preferences of students (Nilsen, Petersen, and Searfoss 1980), how much elaboration children of various age levels employ in their writing

(Loban 1976), or whether male or female characters predominate in basal readers (Rupley, Garcia, and Longnion 1981). In short, any time an investigator is interested in enumerating or measuring the frequencies or relationships of some occurrence or phenomenon, descriptive research techniques will probably be used.

Research reports that employ descriptive methodologies often have a deceptive appearance. They seem easy to understand, even for the non-researcher. While some descriptive studies employ complicated statistical manipulations, complex statistical treatments of data are rare. The apparent simplicity of these reports can be misleading, however. Many factors threaten the reliability, validity, and generalizability of the findings of descriptive studies, which will be discussed in this chapter. Such research must be conducted carefully, with as much rigor as is usually accorded to those studies using more complex research designs. Similarly, descriptive research must be read carefully and critically if the reader is to arrive at a solid understanding of the limitations and implications of these studies.

DATA COLLECTION TECHNIQUES

Surveys and Questionnaires

Many data collection techniques are used in descriptive studies. One popular approach is the use of surveys or questionnaires, which can take many forms, including lists of multiple-choice or open-ended questions or diaries. Survey research usually requires little direct effort on the part of the investigator, which makes it possible to collect information from a large number of subjects. Surveys are often used to find out about opinions or attitudes, although sometimes they are used to access factual information as well (that is, How frequently do you do this? Which books do you employ? Are you required to use this approach?).

The distinction between *attitudinal* or *opinion* information and *objective* information is sometimes blurred when subjects are required to provide objective information that is not readily available or that places much demand on memory. For example, Ruddell and Kinzer (1982) asked both opinion questions and objective information questions of teachers and principals about school testing procedures. Test preference responses indicated that teachers favored the use of criterion-referenced reading tests over standardized tests. This information was gained from questions clearly designed to tap attitudes, opinions, and feelings—phenomena not easily observed. Also, teachers and principals were asked whether test-taking behavior was being taught. This questions was intended to elicit objective information. Nevertheless, 33 percent to 67 percent of the teachers from each school indicated that they did teach test taking, while only 33 percent of the principals drawn from the same schools indicated that this was the case. This disagreement might be due to the fact that the teachers were able to provide factual or objective information ("Yes, I teach test taking"), while the principals were, in many cases, providing opinions only ("I don't actually know, but I don't think they teach that").

Surveys are usually completed anonymously. In fact, anonymity can be one of their major benefits. Subjects are often more willing to share, truthfully, information of a sensitive nature when anonymity is assured. For instance, many teachers might feel uncomfortable reporting on their own instructional efforts or on their attitudes towards school policies if their administrators could find out their responses.

On the other hand, this dependence upon the subjects' efforts also creates an important limitation for survey research: There is always a possibility of a low response rate. The lower the percentage of returned or completed questionnaires, the less dependable the results of the study. Often, those who respond are different in some way from those who do not. This is especially true if the subjects being studied differ very much from each other in terms of the information they can give. A response rate of less than 50 percent is rarely acceptable. When a low response rate is obtained, the investigator should try to mitigate its impact by demonstrating that no relevant differences exist between the respondents and non-respondents.

Gray and Rogers (1956) attempted to find out the purposes of adult reading by eliciting information from subjects drawn from all strata of American society. Of course, not everyone was willing to provide information. This was especially true of those subjects with the least amount of formal education, so the results were apt to overrepresent the purposes of some groups and underrepresent those of others. Therefore, Gray and Rogers tried to reduce this bias by collecting information from a sample that carefully represented the educational and economic status of the nation. If fewer subjects with less than an eighth grade education responded, then more were contacted to keep the ratio correctly balanced.

Interviews

Interviews are also used frequently in descriptive research studies. The interview does not differ greatly from the questionnaire in that the subjects are again expected to provide both attitudinal and factual data. However, in this method, subjects answer questions posed by an interviewer, rather than privately marking their answers themselves. Interviews are demanding of the researcher's time, but the use of interviews often guarantees that more in-depth information will be provided. Subjects have a greater tendency to answer all of the questions when they are interviewed. They are also apt to provide more complete answers because the interviewer is able to ask follow-up questions or to provide necessary clarification when the subject does not understand a question.

Although the interview provides more information, it reduces the benefits of anonymity usually associated with surveys. Subjects are often less willing to provide accurate information in an interview than in an anonymous survey if the information is perceived as being damaging or embarrassing. In fact, sometimes subjects do not answer truthfully; instead, they say what they think the researcher wants them to say.

Observations

Another popular research method common to many descriptive studies is *observation*. This technique is quite different from either the survey or interview methods. First, only objective behavior can be observed; attitudinal information can only be inferred. Also, the subjects do not provide the data in the same way in observational studies that they do in studies using the other, nonobservational methods. Information is obtained directly by the investigator or other trained personnel.

Because the subjects' attitudes and opinions cannot directly bias the data, observational methods often have the appearance of being more objective than other data collection methods. This is doubtful, however. If the characteristics to be observed cannot be reliably noted, then the data may be biased by the researcher's own beliefs or opinions. Also, the act of observation itself—if it is intrusive or perceived as threatening to the subjects—can cause subjects to alter their usual behaviors. For instance, Labov (1970) found that the use of white adult observers led to defensive withdrawal behaviors in many black children. He concluded that this procedure did not permit reasonable estimations of the language proficiency of black children. Descriptive research methods are only useful when they allow an objective description of the actual nature of what is being observed. Any alteration of the phenomena by the data collection itself invalidates the observations.

Objective Tests

It is also possible to administer some type of objective achievement test or performance measure to subjects. This approach allows the researcher to discern the incidence of some knowledge or skill in a population of interest. This technique is not often employed in descriptive studies, but its use has been invaluable in estimating literacy rates. The National Health Survey (1973) administered a standardized reading comprehension test to a national sample of noninstitutionalized youths (12–17 years old). This study defined literacy as "that level of achievement which is attained by the average child in the U.S. at the beginning of the fourth grade" (1973, 1). On the basis of test performance, it was estimated that nearly 5 percent of youths in that age group were illiterate.

The researcher can do similar studies by using archival data, or data that is already available. For example, one study examined standardized reading test scores collected by various school districts from 1950 to 1970

(Farr, Tuinman, and Rowls 1974). These data were used to infer the comparative effectiveness of reading instruction over this period. It was concluded that reading ability had probably increased steadily from 1950 until about 1965, when it began to level off. Of course, as the authors were careful to point out, the confidence that can be placed upon the results of this type of research is limited by the quality of the measures that were originally used.

DISTINGUISHING DESCRIPTIVE RESEARCH

Surveys, interviews, observations, and tests are all used in descriptive research. These techniques can be used, and often are, in other types of studies, too. In order to avoid confusion, as well as to highlight the definition of descriptive research, it is useful to compare and contrast descriptive research with other research approaches.

Ethnography and Descriptive Research

Ethnographies and descriptive studies that employ observational techniques can appear to be strikingly similar. These two types of research are often used to answer the same types of questions, and their results can be nearly identical. Nevertheless, a comparison of ethnographic research (described in chapter 5) and descriptive research (as described here) reveals some important distinctions between these two forms of inquiry.

Descriptive research and ethnographic research both describe, but they stem from different philosophies. In descriptive studies, the investigator decides the questions to be answered and the categories in which to distribute observations prior to data collection. The characteristics of interest are defined a priori. In contrast, pre–data collection decisions are studiously avoided in ethnographic studies, as it is assumed that such preconceptions will lead the investigator to ignore important features of the phenomena being observed. Also, descriptive research will always have a quantitative outcome, even if the results are only reported as frequencies or percentages. On the other hand, ethnographic investigations may report quantitative outcomes, but this is not necessary. Ethnographies often reject the apparent objectivity of quantitative results in favor of a more subjective qualitative analysis by the participant observer.

Experiments and Descriptive Research

Descriptive research can be more easily discerned from experimental investigations. No important manipulation of conditions is appropriate in descriptive research, while experiments manipulate or change the situation in order to reveal causal connections. The act of data collection itself is not considered to be a manipulation, unless it appears that this has influenced the results in some way. For example, if an experimenter wanted to find out the incidence of some behavior during writing, it would be necessary to have subjects do some writing. Having subjects do such writing would only be considered to be a manipulation if the data collection conditions were so different from typical writing conditions that the outcomes were influenced. Descriptive and experimental research are similar in that both are theory based rather than data based. That is, the data collection instruments and categories of analysis are based upon previous research and theory, rather than being an outgrowth of the data collected for that particular study.

Correlational Research and Descriptive Research

Finally, there is a need to compare descriptive research with quasi-experimental studies or correlational investigations. Actually, there is very little difference between these two forms. Sometimes it is claimed that descriptive research describes the nature of events, while correlational research specifies causal connections. This is not a fair distinction, however: It implies that descriptive studies do not attempt to reveal causes, and this is not the case.

For example, the National Assessment of Educational Progress (NAEP 1981a) recently demonstrated that children in American schools are rather limited in a variety of writing abilities. In addition to testing the writing skills of a carefully selected national sample of youngsters, the NAEP study had the students complete a questionnaire about their school writing experiences. It was found that these students had participated in little directed writing activity at school. Thus, the questionnaires provided information that allowed the inference of a reasonable causal explanation (that is, lack of instruction) for the lack of writing sophistication.

Correlations, bivariate or multivariate, are often calculated in descriptive research studies in order to specify the amount of relationship between various measures. Descriptive research is used for measuring the values of naturally occurring variables; such research can also be used to measure relationships between these variables, as long as no manipulation of the environmental features of interest has taken place. For this reason, much correlational and multivariate research is descriptive. (Other aspects of correlational and multivariate research that are beyond the scope of this chapter are discussed in chapters 3 and 8.)

DOING DESCRIPTIVE RESEARCH

In order to better understand descriptive research studies, it is useful to consider how the researcher actually goes about collecting, analyzing, and reporting such data. To conduct descriptive research, an investigator usually follows five general procedures.

1. **Define questions to be answered.**

   The investigator first must establish questions to be answered or hypotheses to be tested. The questions are usually an outgrowth of a sound theoretical base. They might be general initially, but such questions should be refined eventually through recourse to previous research and to the researcher's theoretical position.

2. **Select the appropriate population and sample.**

   Any large group that we may wish to study is called a *population*. A population might be all high school seniors, all elementary school teachers, or all basal readers. Usually it is impossible to examine or observe all of the subjects in a population of interest. For this reason, the researcher is usually interested in examining some *samples* or subsets of the population of interest, from which inferences about the population can be drawn.

   Two types of inferences or generalizations can be made by the researcher: *logical* and *statistical*. Logical generalizations are drawn when the researcher has no direct evidence of the sample's ability to represent the population. Instead, the researcher attempts to use logic or intuition in supporting the generalizability of the evidence collected from the sample. The decision to attempt a logical generalization is usually made on the basis of cost, as it is expensive to examine subjects from all parts of the country. However, logical generalization is most appropriate when the researcher has some reason to believe that there is little variance across subjects in the characteristics or behaviors of interest. If there is a great deal of variance in the population, the researcher runs the risk of selecting a sample that only represents a portion of the population distribution. In cases in which much population variance is expected, it is usually more appropriate to make statistical generalizations.

   Statistical generalizations require some kind of random sampling from the population. Random sampling means that all members of the population have an equal opportunity of being included in the sample actually used for data collection. There are many variants of random sampling. In one of these variants, *stratified* random sampling, subjects are selected randomly but in a way that allows proportions of subgroups within the sample to reflect the proportions of the same subgroups in the population. The researcher might decide, perhaps, that half the sample must have incomes of less than $18,000 per year or that 12 percent of the sample must be black. Survey sampling procedures permit an exact specification of the accuracy of the research findings as a representation of the population. For example, election polls usually indicate that the polling results represent the percentage of voters who support a certain candidate, plus or minus 3 percent. This means that the sample size used in the poll allows a reasonable certainty that a candidate will actually receive a vote percentage in the range of 3 points less than and 3 points more than the percentage observed in the sample. Thus, if a poll reports that 42 percent of a sample favors candidate A, we can be almost certain that the *true* proportion in the population is somewhere between 39 percent and 45 percent.

The researcher must decide whether to attempt logical or statistical generalization. To draw a logical generalization, the researcher simply selects a sample on the basis of intuition, cost, efficiency, and ease of data collection. To draw a statistical generalization, the researcher identifies the approximate size of the population of interest, decides the degree of accuracy required, and then, on the basis of this information, randomly selects a specific number of subjects to participate in the study.

3. Design data collection instruments and establish data collection procedures.

The investigator must decide what type of data collection instruments to use (surveys, interviews, observations, tests, and so on). This decision is made on the basis of the researcher's theory in a way that limits intrusiveness (the influence of methods or procedures upon the outcomes), while maximizing the efficiency and amount of information collected. The researcher designs the actual research instruments and field tests their use prior to the data collection in order to ensure that they can be used validly and reliably. Such field testing should take place in a context similar to that which will be studied. Procedures are then established that dictate exactly how to collect the data. The procedures include deciding, for example, when and how to recontact subjects in survey studies (to ensure maximum response) or days and times to observe, interview, or test subjects.

4. Collect data using the procedures and instruments designed for the study.

If the study uses observations or interviews, it is usually appropriate to retest the procedures periodically to avoid slippage (that is, failure to use the instruments or procedures in a consistent and unbiased fashion).

5. Analyze and consider the data in a variety of ways.

Finally, the researcher must combine the data in a variety of ways to provide the most informative presentation of results possible. For example, information might be collapsed into fewer but more useful categories. Frequencies, percentages, or other relationships might be calculated, or results might be divided to reveal similarities or differences across subsets of the sample studied. For example, Austin and Morrison (1963) reported that 35 percent of reading time in the elementary grades is devoted to oral reading. They went on to provide a grade-level breakdown of this result, which indicated that first- and second-grade teachers focussed on oral reading 67 percent of the time, while teachers in grades five and six did so only about 8 percent of the time.

READING
DESCRIPTIVE RESEARCH REPORTS

Reports of descriptive research differ greatly in scope. Sometimes descriptive studies are reported as portions of larger reports. In such cases, the descriptive section of the paper is intended to provide (1) general background context within which to interpret the remainder of the report, (2) specific baseline data against which eventual treatment effects might be compared, or (3) possible explanations for other results within the same paper. Book-length descriptive studies are common, too.

Readers who are uncertain as to whether or not a report is descriptive in nature should first examine the methodology or procedures section. The methodology section will indicate whether the investigator has manipulated the existing conditions. If there is no manipulation, it is probably a descriptive study. The use of questionnaires, surveys, or interviews also often suggests that the study is descriptive in nature. If no manipulation is apparent, the reader should check to see if the researcher began the investigation with specific research questions. This will help distinguish the report from an ethnography. Finally, the results section of a descriptive research study should be examined. Descriptive studies have a greater tendency than other studies to report frequencies and percentages as the ultimate data-analytic outcome. Nevertheless, more complex analyses (that is, correlations, tests of significance, and so on) might be included in descriptive research studies.

QUESTIONS TO ASK
ABOUT DESCRIPTIVE RESEARCH

The following questions can be used for understanding and evaluating descriptive research reports.

1. Have specific research questions been stated clearly? (What are they?)
2. What are the key terms and concepts used in the study? Have they been defined clearly and appropriately? (State terms and definitions.)
3. Is logical or statistical generalization to be employed? (Which?)
4. What is the population of interest? What sample is to be examined? (Relate them.)
5. Are the data collection *instruments* valid, reliable, and appropriate to the research questions? (Evaluate each.)

6. Are the data collection *procedures* reliable and appropriate to the research questions? (Indicate how the procedures could bias the results.)

7. Are the results stated clearly? (What are they?)

8. Were there missing or incomplete data? Could this have biased the results? (How?)

9. Could the data be reconceptualized or interpreted differently so as to alter the investigator's conclusions? (How?)

10. What relevance does this study have for you?

An Example

The following excerpts are taken from Dolores Durkin's widely cited study, "What Classroom Observations Reveal About Reading Comprehension Instruction" (1978–79). The paper reports the results of three studies that attempt to find, describe, and measure the amount of reading comprehension instruction in reading and social studies classes in grades three through six. Only Durkin's first study will be examined here. Durkin presents the following information:

> As a veteran observer of elementary school classrooms, I was especially struck by the second assumption [Reading comprehension is being taught] because my frequent visits to schools have revealed almost no comprehension instruction. Two facts could have accounted for this, however. First, comprehension instruction never was the preselected focus for an observation and, second, the bulk of the observing was in primary grades. (1978–79, 483)
>
> . . . I decided to see what conclusions would be reached if middle- and upper-grade classrooms were observed for the purpose of finding, describing, and timing comprehension instruction. (1978–79, 484)
>
> In order to look at comprehension instruction from a variety of perspectives, 3 sub-studies were done. One concentrated on fourth grade because it is commonly believed that at that level a switch is made from *learning to read* to *reading to learn*. It is also at that level that content subjects begin to be taken seriously. These 2 factors, it was thought, made fourth grade a likely place to find comprehension instruction. (1978–79, 494)

> *Have specific research questions been stated clearly?*
> *What are they?*

Durkin has clearly defined specific research questions. These questions were formulated prior to data collection on the basis of her knowledge and beliefs, or a priori. They did not emerge as a result of the research itself.

What are the key terms and concepts used in the study?
Have they been defined clearly and appropriately?
Are the terms defined unambiguously or would you have difficulty recognizing examples of each?

Durkin arrived at several specific definitions after a thorough review of the literature, including an examination of basic articles and textbooks and previous studies of comprehension instruction and time use in the classroom. Durkin had to create her own definitions of comprehension instruction, because she found none in her literature review. She provided specific definitions, a rationale for each, and examples of behaviors that would represent each term. Some of the definitions include:

> *Comprehension: instruction*—Teacher does/says something to help children understand or work out the meaning of more than a single, isolated word. . . .
> *Comprehension: application*—Teacher does/says something in order to learn whether previous instruction enables children to understand the meaning of connected text not used in that instruction. (1978–79, 488)
> *Comprehension: assessment*—Teacher does/says something in order to learn whether what was read was comprehended. Efforts could take a variety of forms—for instance, orally posed questions; written exercises; request for picture of unpictured character in a story. (1978–79, 490)
> *Comprehension: assignment*—Teacher gives written assignment concerned with comprehension. . . .
> *Comprehension: helps with assignment*—Teacher helps one or more children with comprehension assignment. . . .
> *Comprehension: review of instruction*—Teacher goes over earlier comprehension instruction. . . .
> *Comprehension: preparation for reading*—Teacher does/says something in order to prepare children to read a given selection—for instance, identifies or has children identify new words; poses questions; relates children's experiences to selection; discusses meanings of words in selection. . . .

Comprehension: prediction—Teacher asks for prediction based on what was read. (1978–79, 491)

Non-instruction—Time given to chastisement; to waiting while children do assignments; to checking papers at desk while children do an assignment; to non-instructional conversation with one or more children, and so on. (1978–79, 493)

> *Is a logical or statistical generalization to be employed? Which?*
> *Is this a reasonable approach?*
> *What is the population of interest?*
> *What sample is to be examined?*

When using statistical generalization, investigators will describe the survey sampling procedures used. Such issues as size of population, probability of sample selection, and optimization of sample size are discussed in such studies. Reports attempting logical generalizations ignore such issues. Instead, the investigator explains rationally why a particular sample represents the population.

Durkin has chosen logical generalization as her approach. She has selected a group of teachers that, she argues, would be expected to provide much comprehension instruction. As she explained in her introduction, little variance in the amount or type of comprehension instruction usually provided in elementary schools was noted; hence, this approach is probably reasonable. Also, the teachers did not know exactly which classroom phenomena were being observed.

In addition to these precautions, Durkin exercised a great deal of care in selecting a model sample. She observed what would be presumed to be better-than-average instruction. Thus, Durkin was able to observe a relatively small number of lessons in order to represent adequately the entire population of minutes of elementary reading instruction.

> The primary reason for the observational study was to learn whether elementary school classrooms provide comprehension instruction and, if they do, to find out what amount of time is allotted to it. On the assumption that there is less of it in the primary grades because of the concern there for decoding skills, middle and upper grades were selected for the observations. (1978–79, 493)

> In all 3 sub-studies, each classroom was visited on 3 successive days. This procedure was followed to allow for continuity and also to reduce the likelihood that teachers would only be seen on an atypical day. On the assumption that both the content and

the quality of instruction varies on different days of the week, the 3-day visits were scheduled so that all 5 days of the week would be included with equal frequency by the time the research terminated. On the assumption that the quality of an instructional program also varies at different times in the school year, observations began in early September and continued until mid-May. (1978–79, 494)

To be noted, too, is that whenever an administrator was contacted about the possibility of observing, a request was made to see the best teachers. While there is no guarantee that the best (which would have different meaning for different administrators) were seen, it is likely that the worst were not seen. Although each teacher knew about the observer's interest in reading, the special interest in comprehension instruction was never mentioned. . . .

Another relevant fact needs to be mentioned. Because observations could only be made with a teacher's permission, times when instruction might be reduced both in quality and in quantity were omitted from the observation schedule. Teachers and/or administrators did not permit visiting, for example, at the very beginning of the school year, or at the very end. Nor were teachers willing to be observed during the weeks that preceded Thanksgiving and Christmas. Even days like Halloween and Valentine's Day had to be omitted. All this is to say that what was seen should have been examples of fairly good instructional programs. (1978–79, 495)

In the study of fourth grades, reading was observed for 4,469 minutes; social studies, for 2,775 minutes. The 24 classrooms that were visited were in 13 different school systems in central Illinois. All the classes were taught by women, 7 of whom had aides. Six of the 24 classes were third-fourth grade combinations. (1978–79, 497)

Are the data collection instruments and procedures valid, reliable,
and appropriate to the research questions?
Could the procedures have biased the results?

Durkin's definitions of terminology constitute, to a great degree, the instrumentation of the study. This was an observational study, so Durkin goes on to describe the training procedures employed to ensure accuracy and consistency. Although the definitions appear to be distinct enough that various activities could be correctly categorized, Durkin indicates that there were initially some problems with the procedures.

In studies such as these, it is usually accepted practice to provide some estimate of *interrater reliability* (consistency of measurement across observers) and *intrarater reliability* (consistency of a single observer over time). These reliabilities are reported as correlation coefficients; reliabilities of less than 0.90 are usually indicative of an instrument that will have inconsistent results. Unfortunately, Durkin provides no clear indication of the interrater or intrarater reliabilities of her procedures, although some effort (post-observation discussion) was made to reduce slippage as the study progressed.

It is to be expected that persons will alter their behaviors when being observed. However, this study protected against such threats to validity by observing teachers over a long period of time and by not informing them of the categories of information being collected. Nevertheless, some information was provided concerning changes of behavior that did occur as a result of the observation. In fact, observation may have caused an increase in the actual amount of instruction provided.

> All the observations were made by this researcher and 2 assistants, who had been prepared to be observers in a number of ways. To begin, both had had elementary school teaching experience; both had also taken reading methodology courses with this writer and had themselves taught an undergraduate course in reading. Before the observations started, time was spent on descriptions and illustrations of each category; directions for recording what was observed were carefully outlined, too.
>
> When a teacher was the focus, recording sheets had the following headings:

Time	Activity	Audience	Source

> The time that each different activity began and ended was noted in the first column, which was also used to indicate how an activity was classified. The second column was for descriptions of each activity. Who was with the teacher at the time of an activity was named in the third column (for example, whole class, small group, single child, principal, etc.) The fourth column allowed for information about the source of an activity—for instance, a workbook or

manual. Only the headings "Time" and "Activity" were used when a child was being observed.

Careful preparation may account for the identical classifications of activities by the observers during 4 trial observations. Two problems were identified, however. With 1 observer, a consistent error in timing activities occurred during the first trial observation because, instead of marking the starting time of an activity to correspond with the concluding time of the previous activity, she skipped a minute. For example, if the categories *transition* and *comprehension: preparation* described 2 successive activities of a teacher, the first of which ended at 9.06, she erroneously noted the second as starting at 9.07 instead of 9.06.

Another observer's reporting was unnecessarily detailed in its accounts of behavior. To remedy that, distinctions had to be made between what was essential and, in contrast, what could be recorded *if* time permitted.

Originally, a minute was considered the basic unit of time. However, as the observations proceeded, some activities were so brief as to require descriptions that used half minutes.

For all 3 sub-studies, every description and classification was checked by this researcher. Unclear descriptions or questionable classifications were discussed with the observer. Questionable classifications, which were uncommon, were resolved through discussions of the given behavior or—and this occurred more frequently—through the addition of categories. All added categories were used infrequently; they included: *sustained silent reading* (both teacher and children are engaged in silent reading); *diagnosis: checks* (teacher looks over sheet on which notes about problems are written); *diagnosis: writes* (teacher makes a notation about a problem or need). (1978–79, 495–97)

> *Are the results stated clearly?*
> *What are they?*
> *Were there missing or incomplete data?*
> *Did this bias the results?*

Durkin reports her data in percentages of time spent observing each activity. She uses a variety of tables and provides clear explanations of each. Because of the nature of her study, there were no missing data.

The amount of time the 24 observed teachers spent during the reading period on instruction and activities concerned with comprehension and study skills is summarized in Table 1 [see Table 4–1]. As the table shows, less than 1 per cent (28 minutes) went to comprehension instruction. At no time was study skills instruction seen. (1978–79, 497)

To describe how the observed teachers did spend their time, Table 4 [see Table 4–2] lists all the categories showing total percentages of 4 or more. Three categories in Table 4 [Table 4–2] have not yet been mentioned but, combined, they consumed almost 31 percent of the teacher's time. The 3 are *non-instruction, transition,* and *listens: to oral reading.*

Non-instruction describes the times when a teacher was doing such things as chastising, talking about something that had no academic value (e.g., a bus schedule), doing nothing while the children worked on assignments, or correcting papers at her

Table 4–1
Percentage of teacher time spent on comprehension and study skills during the reading period

Behavioral Categories	Percentage of 4,469 Minutes
Comprehension: instruction	0.63
Comprehension: review of instruction	N.O.[a]
Comprehension: application	N.O.
Comprehension: assignment	2.13
Comprehension: help with assignment	5.46
Comprehension: preparation for reading	5.53
Comprehension: assessment	17.65
Comprehension: prediction	0.25
Study skills: instruction	N.O.
Study skills: review of instruction	N.O.
Study skills: application	0.43
Study skills: assignment	0.16
Total	32.24

[a]N.O. = not observed
Source: Durkin 1978–79, 498. Reprinted with permission of the author and the International Reading Association.

Table 4–2
Categories for the reading periods with largest percentages of time allotted to them

Behavioral Categories	Percentage of 4,469 Minutes
Comprehension: assessment	17.65
Noninstruction	10.72
Transition	10.47
Listens: to oral reading	9.76
Assignment: help with	6.94
Comprehension: preparation for reading	5.53
Comprehension: help with assignment	5.46
Assignment: gives	4.72

Source: Durkin 1978–79, 502. Reprinted with permission of the author and the International Reading Association.

desk. The largest contributor to the 10.72 percentage figure shown for *non-instruction* was "correcting papers at desk." Frequently they were math papers. While this writer was surprised at the frequency with which teachers were willing to sit at their desk correcting papers while an observer was in the room, it is possible that they would have been there with even greater frequency if a visitor had not been present. This is suggested by the fact that more correcting went on when the research assistants were observing than when this writer was the observer. (1978–79, 501–502).

Could the data be reconceptualized so as to alter the investigator's conclusions?
What relevance does this study have?

Could the categories in Durkin's study be recombined so as to have somewhat less pessimistic results? Hodges (1980), in a commentary on Durkin's article, criticizes the separation of some of the categories, such as teacher question asking from comprehension instruction question asking. When Hodges combined these categories on the basis of a broader definition of *comprehension instruction,* she found that more than 23 percent of the time was spent in comprehension instruction, as opposed to Durkin's finding of less than 1 percent.

A recombination of categories indicates that there is substantially more comprehension instruction than Durkin claims. Durkin defines *comprehension instruction* as requiring direct explanation or telling. Hodges views *instruction* as being less directive than that; she was thus able to find more instruction reflected in Durkin's figures.

In either case, one could argue that little comprehension instruction—by either definition—is taking place in classrooms, where it should be a major focus. Therefore, Durkin's study exposes an important deficiency in classroom instructional practice. It also encourages us to examine this aspect of our own teaching more carefully and to search for ways of alleviating the problem. But it does not tell us why there is so little comprehension instruction, nor does it identify the actual impact of this limited amount of instruction.

FINDINGS OF DESCRIPTIVE STUDIES

Descriptive studies, such as Durkin's, have provided a great deal of information concerning reading and writing. Such studies have provided important information about achievement levels, instructional practices, and the nature of cognitive processes in reading and writing. We will examine findings from descriptive research studies briefly here in order to illustrate descriptive research results.

Achievement Levels

Descriptive research has been able to provide estimates of literacy and achievement rates. For example, the National Assessment of Educational Progress (NAEP 1979; 1981a) has periodically tested carefully selected national samples (using survey sampling procedures) of 9-, 13-, and 17-year-old students in a variety of achievement areas. Such studies have produced reasonable estimates of reading and writing abilities; they have permitted an examination of changes in these achievement levels over time, also. The NAEP studies have suggested a rather slight improvement in reading ability and a slight decline in writing ability during the 1970s. The latest NAEP data, however, suggest that the gains in reading might be due to improvements in the ability to answer multiple-choice questions only. Students seem to be "satisfied with their initial interpretations of what they read and seem genuinely puzzled at requests to explain or defend their points of view" (NAEP 1981b, 2). Students were found to be unable to elaborate, interpret, or explain their evaluations of reading material. Similarly, students declined in their ability to write persuasive papers or narratives. Findings such as these can help educators develop better instructional objectives and determine the effectiveness of current policies.

Instructional Practices

Descriptive studies can also provide information about instructional practices. Several studies have examined writing instruction in the elementary grades. For example, in a survey study, Shanahan (1979) found that teachers claimed to provide only about 30 minutes of writing instruction (including student writing time) per week in the elementary grades. Many teachers did not even know whether they were supposed to teach writing! This study also found that teacher's objectives for teaching writing exerted virtually no influence upon the instructional and evaluative procedures that they said they used. Another survey study (Petty and Finn 1981) reported similar findings concerning the amount of writing instruction. Students were rarely asked to write letters, essays, directions, news articles, or announcements; most student writing took the form of stories. Similarly, only about 7 percent of elementary and high school students reported that they regularly created multiple drafts for writing assignments or that they received written or oral comments about their writing from teachers (NAEP 1981a). Such studies highlight areas of instruction that can be enhanced and imply possible ways that such improvement can be achieved.

Relationships of Teaching and Learning

Descriptive studies can also offer important information about the nature of learning and its relationship to a variety of instructional practices. For example, the Beginning Teacher Evaluation Study (Fisher et al. 1978) found that the amount of academic learning time (ALT) provided to students was significantly related to reading achievement. ALT is defined as the time a student is engaged with activities that yield high achievement (that is, guided practice, reading appropriate level of material, and so on). Stallings (1980) has extended this work into secondary remedial reading classes. She found higher achievement in classes that balanced the amount of reading, discussion, and writing time than in those that required a preponderance of reading or writing.

The influence of reading curriculum (Barr 1974; Calfee and Piontkowski 1981) upon reading strategies has also been measured using descriptive techniques. These studies found that first-graders, who received different types of reading instruction (meaning based, decoding based) had different conceptions of reading and used different reading strategies. Essentially, beginning readers attempted to use the approach stressed instructionally; but, as they acquired literacy, they came to use meaning-based (context, word recall) *and* decoding-based strategies (syllabication, phonics) in an integrated fashion.

Process Description

Descriptive research has been used frequently in recent years to describe the process of writing. Such studies have used think-aloud protocol analysis or observation. In the think-aloud procedure, subjects are asked to tell what they are doing as they write. The researcher records the subjects' statements and examines them in relationship to the writing produced. These data are not simply observed; they are organized on the basis of the researcher's theory in order to make sense of how someone writes.

In one study, Hayes and Flower (1980) examined the think-alouds of adults who were doing expository writing and found that writing is a three-part process made up of planning, translating, and reviewing. Editing, which is treated as a culminating activity in many instructional manuals, is done during all three parts of the process, not just in the final one. In addition, Flower and Hayes (1981) found that writers generate a variety of writing plans that attend to content, style, tone, readers' needs, and even typographical form of the final product. These methods are very different from the straightforward outlining procedures often included in instructional materials.

Matsuhashi (1981) also has attempted to describe how writers write. Instead of using think-aloud protocols, she has observed the physical act of writing, paying particular attention to the pauses that writers make. By examining these pauses, along with the nature of the text produced after these pauses, Matsuhashi has provided a valuable description of the on-going decision making that takes place during writing. Such information is potentially useful for discovering the locus of writing difficulty that could allow better instruction.

IN SUMMARY

Descriptive research attempts to describe characteristics, properties, or relationships of groups, events, or phenomena. Several techniques of data collection (surveys, questionnaires, interviews, observations, and so on) can be used in descriptive research. However, no matter what procedures are used, manipulation or alteration of the phenomena of interest must be avoided. The intention is to describe accurately the nature and relationships of events.

Descriptive research data can be used to provide simple descriptions of events. This approach is especially useful for increasing awareness of a particular problem or for providing baseline data for future work. Descriptive research data can also be used to allow logical causal inferences to be drawn. Descriptive research studies in reading and writing have provided invaluable estimates of achievement levels and useful status reports on classroom instruction.

REFERENCES

Austin, M. C., & Morrison, C. (1963). *The first r.* New York: Macmillan.

Barr, R. C. (1974). The effect of instruction on pupil reading strategies. *Reading Research Quarterly, 10,* 555–582.

Calfee, R. C., & Piontkowski, D. C. (1981). The reading diary: Acquisition of decoding. *Reading Research Quarterly, 16,* 346–373.

Durkin, D. (1978–79). What classroom observations reveal about reading comprehension instruction. *Reading Research Quarterly, 14,* 481–533.

Farr, R., Tuinman, J., & Rowls, M. (1974). *Reading achievement in the United States: THEN and NOW.* Bloomington, IN: The Reading Program Center and the Institute for Child Study, Indiana University.

Fisher, C. W., Filby, N. N., Marliave, R., Cahen, L. S., Dishaw, M. M., Moore, J. E., & Berliner, D. C. (1978). *Teaching behaviors, academic learning time, and student achievement* (Final Report of Phase III-B Beginning Teacher Evaluation Study). San Francisco: Far West Laboratory for Educational Research and Development.

Flower, L. S., & Hayes, J. R. (1981). Plans that guide the composing process. In C. H. Frederickson & J. F. Dominic (Eds.), *Writing: The nature, development and teaching of written communication* (2nd ed., pp. 39–58). Hillsdale, NJ: Erlbaum.

Gray, W. S., & Rogers, B. (1956). *Maturity in reading.* Chicago: University of Chicago Press.

Hayes, J. R., & Flower, L. S. (1980). Identifying the organization of writing processes. In L. W. Gregg & E. R. Steinberg (Eds.), *Cognitive processes in writing* (pp. 3–30). Hillsdale, NJ: Erlbaum.

Hodges, C. A. (1980). Commentary: Toward a broader definition of comprehension instruction. *Reading Research Quarterly, 15,* 299–306.

Labov, W. (1970). The logic of nonstandard English. In J. E. Alatis (Ed.), *20th annual round table* (pp. 1–39). Washington, D.C.: Georgetown University Press.

Loban, W. (1976). *Language development.* Urbana, IL: National Council of Teachers of English.

Matsuhashi, A. (1981). Pausing and planning: The tempo of written discourse production. *Research in the Teaching of English, 15,* 113–134.

NAEP. (1979). *Reading change, 1970–75: Summary volume.* Denver: National Assessment of Educational Progress.

NAEP. (1981a). *Writing achievement, 1969–79* (Vols. 1–3). Denver: National Assessment of Educational Progress.

NAEP. (1981b). *Reading, thinking and writing.* Denver: National Assessment of Educational Progress.

National Health Survey. (1973). *Literacy among youth 12–17 years: United States.* Washington, D.C.: U.S. Department of Health, Educational and Welfare, Series II, No. 131, H.E. 20.6209.

Nilsen, A. P., Peterson, R., & Searfoss, L. W. (1980). The adult as critic vs. the child as reader. *Language Arts, 57,* 530–539.

Petty, W. T., & Finn, P. J. (1981). Classroom teachers' reports on teaching written composition. In S. Haley-James (Ed.), *Perspectives on writing in grades 1–8* (pp. 19–34). Urbana, IL: National Council of Teachers of English.

Ruddell, R., & Kinzer C. (1982). Test preferences and competencies of field educators. In J. A. Niles & L. A. Harris (Eds.), *New inquiries in reading research and instruction* (Thirty-first Yearbook of the National Reading Conference, pp. 196–199). Rochester, NY: National Reading Conference.

Rupley, W. H., Garcia, J., & Longnion, B. (1981). Sex role portrayal in reading materials: Implications for the 1980's. *Reading Teacher, 34,* 786–791.

Shanahan, T. (1979). The writing crisis: A survey and solution. *Kappan, 61,* 216–217.

Stallings, J. (1980). Allocated academic learning time revisited, or beyond time on task. *Educational Researcher, 9,* 11–16.

ADDITIONAL SOURCES
OF DESCRIPTIVE RESEARCH PROCEDURES

Babbie, E. R. (1973). *Survey research methods.* Belmont, CA: Wadsworth.

Cochran, W. G. (1977). *Sampling techniques* (3rd ed). New York: Wiley.

Guilford, J. P. (1954). *Psychometric methods* (2nd ed.). New York: McGraw-Hill.

Kidder, L. H. (1981). *Sellitz, Wrightsman & Cook's research methods in social relations* (4th ed.). New York: Holt, Rinehart and Winston.

Kish, L. (1965). *Survey sampling.* New York: Wiley.

Nisbet, J. S., & Entwistle, N. J. (1970). *Educational research methods.* New York: American Elsevier.

Pohl, N. F., & Bruno, A. V. (1978). Reducing item specific non-response bias. *Journal of Experimental Education, 46,* 57–64.

Rosenberg, M. (1968). *The logic of survey analyses.* New York: Basic Books.

Schuman, H., & Presser, S. (1981). *Questions and answers in attitude surveys.* New York: Academic Press.

ADDITIONAL EXAMPLES
OF DESCRIPTIVE STUDIES

Applebee, A. (1981). *Writing in the secondary school.* Urbana, IL: National Council of Teachers of English.

Calfee, R. C., & Drum, P. A. (Eds.). (1979). *Teaching reading in compensatory classes.* Newark, DE: International Reading Association.

Cipolla, C. M. (1969). *Literacy and development in the west.* Baltimore: Penguin Books.

Fisher, C. J., & Natarella, M. A. (1982). Young children's preferences in poetry: A national survey of first, second, and third graders. *Research in the Teaching of English, 16,* 339–354.

Hiebert, E. H. (1981). Developmental patterns and interrelationships of preschool children's print awareness. *Reading Research Quarterly, 16,* 236–260.

Leinhardt, G., Zigmond, N., & Cooley, W. W. (1981). Reading instruction and its effects. *American Educational Research Journal, 18,* 343–361.

Morrison, C., & Austin, M. C. (1977). *The torch lighters revisited.* Newark, DE: International Reading Association.

Northcutt, N. W. (1975). *Adult functional competency: A summary*. Austin: University of Texas.

Ninio, A. (1980). Picture-book reading in mother-infant dyads belonging to two subgroups in Israel. *Child Development, 51,* 587–590.

O'Donnell, R. C., Griffin, W. J., & Norris, R. C. (1967). *Syntax of kindergarten and elementary school children: A transformational analysis.* Champaign, IL: National Council of Teachers of English.

Sharon, A. T. (1973–74). What do adults read? *Reading Research Quarterly, 9,* 148–169.

Chapter 5

Ethnographic
Methodologies

In its broadest sense, *naturalistic inquiry* is the method of research that considers how the experience of an individual, group, or society is influenced by and, in turn, influences its surrounding context. It is field based rather than laboratory based; that is, it requires that behavior be examined in natural settings.

Ethnographic research has become one of the major naturalistic alternatives to experimental methodologies. This chapter will focus on what ethnographic research is, what underlying principles shape its methods, and how it differs from experimental research. (Descriptive/observational and case study research were discussed in chapter 4.)

Figure 5–1 outlines some of the major distinctions between experimental and ethnographic inquiry. While the experimental-naturalistic contrast is always a matter of degree, rather than a statement of opposite poles, the experimental-ethnographic contrast is much more distinct, emanating from differing philosophical views. Experimental inquiry is generally based on a positivist view of social behavior (Comte 1973; Durkheim 1956) that seeks to identify facts and causes. Ethnographic inquiry emanates from a phenomenological base (Husserl 1931; Schutz 1970; Weber 1947) that seeks to understand social behavior from the participants' frames of reference. This distinction is at the core of the differences between the methodologies and must be recognized in order to understand how each approach necessitates adherence to its own methodologically consistent principles of data gathering and verification.

Most of the experimental designs used in reading and writing research were adapted from the physical and biological sciences and seek to understand behavior by testing relationships between or among variables (see

Figure 5–1
Major distinctions between ethnographic and experimental inquiry

Ethnographic Inquiry	Experimental Inquiry
A. Phenomenological base: Seeks to understand human behavior from the participants' frame of reference	A. Positivist base: Seeks to learn facts and identify causes
B. Systematically observes recurring patterns of behavior as people engage in regularly occurring activities	B. Sets variables that need to be understood in relation to each other—some (independent) can be manipulated to determine their effects on others (dependent)
C. Identifies and describes phenomena from beginning to end across cycles	C. Tests relationships
D. Develops hypotheses grounded in the event and driven by the conceptual framework of the study	D. Preformulates research questions or hypotheses
E. Uses field settings that can be further tested with naturalistic experiments	E. Uses laboratory or field settings
F. Confirms findings across a variety of information sources, contexts, and time	F. Computes interrater agreement and statistical probability

chapters 6 and 7). Ethnographic inquiry in these areas has its roots in the field of anthropology and is concerned with understanding behavior through the process of generating a conceptual framework from data gathered in field settings. Preformulated questions or hypotheses are carefully avoided in this form of naturalistic inquiry, since they may, potentially, limit the scope of observations and interpretations. However, observations are not at random; they are grounded in and driven by the empirical evidence. This grounding is reflected in the way researchers take field notes, record observations, and devise models. While statistical procedures are not precluded from ethnographic studies, they tend to be used in only a small portion of the work. However, the real issue is *when* and *what* rather than *whether* to quantify.

ETHNOGRAPHIC INQUIRY

The term *ethnography* was first used by Malinowski in 1922 and refers to the anthropological process of studying a whole culture. An ethnography is a description of what a culture *is*, what being a member of that culture *means*, and how that culture *differs* from other cultures. An ethnography is the product of systematic observations, interviews, and case histories. Emphasis is on obtaining detailed descriptions of processes and interactions that occur as people engage in everyday activities within and across a variety of settings—on describing natural interrelationships among people, among events, and between people and events. A major aspect of naturalistic inquiry is its adherence to the notion of ecological validity (Bronfenbrenner 1976), which suggests that behavior should be studied in its regularly occurring time, place, and situation. This permits the natural balance of intervening variables to be maintained.

Educational ethnography seeks to understand the culture of the educational or learning process: (1) what is occurring, (2) how it is occurring, (3) how the participants perceive the event, (4) what is required to participate as a member of that educational group (play group, reading group, class, and so on), and (5) what social and academic learning takes place.

Not all educational ethnography seeks to understand social interaction or face-to-face micro levels of behavior. Some ethnographic research focuses on patterns of interaction on a macro level between individuals, groups, and institutions, or institutions with institutions (for example, Ogbu 1978). The problem in the development of an educational ethnography is that educational institutions such as homes or schools are only segments of the whole. They are not fully representative of and cannot account for the many influences that affect behavior in the life of a child. Therefore, many educational ethnographers not only observe communicative interactions within the school setting, but also immerse themselves in the home culture in order to describe a wider range of factors that affect the students' perceptions of schooling and learning. Others conduct an in-depth study of parts (class, event, day, week, school) and seek to understand these parts in depth within an ever-increasing whole.

Both macro- and microethnographies describe cycles of events that have been observed to occur regularly across time. A holistically viewed unit may be a community, a school system, or the beginning of one lesson in a single classroom. To provide the necessary unity, ethnographers need to lay out the parameters of what is to be studied—to define the unit of analysis to be considered as the whole. To illustrate the differences and the knowledge to be gained, two ethnographic studies will be considered: Philips' work on Warm Springs schools and home cultures, and Erickson and his colleagues' (Schultz and Florio) on classroom events.

Philips (1972), in an early and influential study, concentrated on the contrast between home and school learning in order to understand the school behavior of reservation-reared Native American children. Through ethnographic techniques, Philips found that the children participated more enthusiastically and effectively in classes that minimized the teacher's control of their performance styles and also minimized teacher attention to their errors. Philips found that these preferences reflected the relationships Native American children were used to at home where support networks of children were extremely important, where peers were not singled out, and where peer relationships provided stronger support systems than adult-child relationships.

This study highlights ways in which we can come to understand that what is communicated in the classroom is a result of the the complex interaction of educational goals, background knowledge, and student perceptions about what is taking place. While the Native American children originally displayed negative behavior (in the eyes of the teacher) and low achievement (in school tasks), an understanding of the students' perception of classroom interactions can permit important changes in classroom organization and interaction, leading, in turn, to changes in student participation and involvement.

Philips' macroethnographic data-gathering techniques can be contrasted with Erickson's (1977) microethnographic techniques. These micro techniques are used to describe what is required to participate in a circumscribed school-based social situation or event (such as a lesson), as opposed to a larger segment of the culture. This technique requires that the researcher identify the parameters of the situation being observed, limiting observations to interactions within the parameters.

For example, Schultz and Florio (1979), building on the work of Erickson, used microethnographic techniques to describe how kindergarteners acquire school social competence. Because they looked at verbal and nonverbal behaviors exhibited during worktime and junctures between activities, it was essential that they carefully define the physical and social communicative space (the targets of their study) during and between activities to ensure observations of all potential communicative interactions within the consistent micro unit. Schultz and Florio found that there are distinct physical and spatial messages that help the students and teacher cooperate to understand aspects of worktime.

When the teacher made announcements or moved during worktime, recurring student behavior was observed, illustrating the communication pattern of the class. For example, the circle area in the kindergarten room was found to take on a sphere of control not felt in any other part of the room. During circle time itself, the teacher is usually the center of attention. However, Schultz and Florio observed that even when children were scattered around the room, if the teacher stepped into the space where the circle usually met, she easily regained their attention by asking the children to freeze. This behavior did not occur in other parts of the room. In this study, Schultz and Florio demonstrated the orderly fashion in which classroom behaviors are developed and reinforced via verbal and nonverbal communication patterns that recur over a period of time. A kindergartener's failure to interpret the inherent social meaning in the teacher's use of movement and space might be a function of miscommunication that needs to be changed by reappraisal of the basic communication pattern. This study is an example of how certain education-related questions can be explored through the use of microethnographic techniques that permit intensive observation of a specific unit of the classroom culture.

As in each of the studies above, an ethnography describes: (1) the context or environment, (2) the group membership (participant or non-participant), (3) the specific social interactions, and (4) the products of those interactions—that is, the actual learning. Said another way, an ethnography defines the group, what it means to be a member of that group, and what happens through participation in that particular group.

In doing ethnographic research, the researcher must remain free from either formal or informal expectations about what is occurring and why. Ethnographers *describe* rather than *judge* what is occurring. They carefully consider the recurring patterns of behavior and infer the rules for participation and membership; thereby, they understand the nature of the interactions and concomitant learning.

In ethnographic research, as in all formalized inquiry, implicit procedures guide the methodology. Six general ethnographic procedures are described below. Since the theory is driven by the data, these steps can be mixed, matched, cycled, and recycled in a variety of ways, depending upon the developing framework.

To do an ethnography a researcher must . . .

1. Define the analytic whole.

In defining the analytic whole, the locus of observation is identified in two ways: reference to previous ethnographic work and use of new observations of recurring events. This permits focus on interactions within the given context and excludes those not included in the prescribed whole. (At times, this step occurs after the initial search of indices.)

2. Use one or more ethnographic methods.

Methods of ethnographic data gathering include participant observation, informant interviews, case histories, life studies, and field notes. Several methods of data gathering are typically used, allowing *triangulation* (verifying by independent and different methods) on behaviors of interest, which are selected based on the need for a more focussed or varied locus of observation.

3. Search for recurring patterns and events.

After the field notes have been prepared, the recordings transcribed and indexed, the video tape coded and thoroughly analyzed, recurring patterns of behavior are used to formulate hypotheses or develop typical case models that are grounded in the data.

4. Validate the findings by regrounding procedures, such as repeated searches through the data, repeated participant observations or interviews, replication of observations, or interviews with other members of the culture on the site or at a similar site. This repeated grounding across data sources and across time validates the findings.

5. Refine models and hypotheses based on regrounding and integrate with previous knowledge.

6. Use the hypotheses and typical case models for later observations and descriptions in similar situations.

Finally, the model can be refined based on the reactions of the participants or applications to other contexts and used for later observations and descriptions within and across situations.

READING ETHNOGRAPHIC REPORTS

Because ethnographic studies tend to provide a vast amount of descriptive information, complete findings are sometimes reported in book form (Heath 1983; Scollon and Scollon 1981; Ogbu 1978). Articles from such studies often present only portions of the data or an abbreviated version of a complete study. At other times, a complete study is presented in a journal article. Frequently, studies are sufficiently rich in data that a number of different articles focus on different aspects of the same study. Therefore, readers of an ethnography and articles from ethnographic studies are faced with the task of determining whether or not what they are reading is the report of the *full study* or merely a *part* of it, and whether what they are reading meets general definitions of an adequate ethnography.

QUESTIONS FOR READING ETHNOGRAPHIC RESEARCH

The following questions can serve as a checklist for understanding and evaluating ethnographic research reports and as a guide to researchers in communicating important information to their readers.

1. Has the goal of the ethnography been clearly stated? (What is it?)
2. Have the parameters of the context been clearly stated? (State them.)
3. Have data been obtained from varying frameworks within the context? (State them.)
4. Have one or more ethnographic methods been used? (Identify them.)
5. Have the recurrent patterns (for example, group membership) been described? (Relate them.)
6. Have the goals of the interactions been described from one or more points of view? (Which?)
7. Have the products of the interactions been described from one or more points of view? (Which?)
8. Has the developing model been described? (What is it?)
9. Have the descriptions been regrounded? (How?)
10. What relevance does this study have for you?

An Example

The following excerpts are from "Questioning at Home and at School: A Comparative Study," by Shirley Brice Heath. (It appears as a chapter in *Doing Ethnography: Educational Anthropology in Action* [1982], edited by George Spindler.) This research describes the uses of questions in three different parts of the same city: a working-class community of black residents, the classrooms of target pupils, and the homes of the teachers. Heath used this study to show how ethnographic data on verbal strategies in home and community settings can be useful for comparison with language data collected in the classroom and as a basis for improving classroom interactions. Early in her paper, she presents the following information:

> The fieldwork reported in this paper was carried out over a period of five years in both community and institutional settings. Results of the work were shared with both community and institutional members. One phase of the fieldwork was done in all-black residential group whose members identified themselves as a community both spatially and in terms of group mem-

bership. To distinguish this group from the public community at large, we will hereafter refer to it as Trackton. Over the period of time in which I worked there, its membership declined from 150 to 40, as families moved from the neighborhood into public housing or purchased new homes. Most Trackton households contained one or more members, aged 21 to 45, who worked in jobs providing salaries equal to or above those of beginning public school teachers in the region; however, jobs were seasonal, and work was not always steady. Trackton was located in a Southeastern city with a population of approximately 40,000; in the period from 1970 to 1975, children from the community attended either of two public elementary-level schools. As a volunteer neighborhood service aide, I worked in these schools and with city personnel in a variety of agencies, collecting data on interactions of Trackton residents in institutions with which they came in frequent, if not daily, contact. As a professor at a state teacher-training institution for which the region's citizens had a long-standing respect, I had many of the teachers, their spouses, or other family members in class, and I worked informally with others on local civic or church-related projects. Over the years, I became colleague, co-author, aide, and associate to many of the classroom teachers, and I had access to not only their classrooms, but also their homes and their activities in the public domain.

I began working in Trackton at the request of some of the older residents who had known me for several years. My initial task, in their view, was to read and talk with the children and explain to adults why their children were not doing better in school.

> *Does it tell the reader about the goal of the ethnography?*
> *What parameters of the contexts are discussed?*
> *If not, what are they?*
> *What does the reader still need to know in order to understand the*
> *background of the study?*

While the above segment describes the parameters of the context, as well as the goal of the ethnography as seen by the residents, we still need to know more about Heath's goals. Heath goes on to describe the manner in which she gained the trust of the community members, how she was called to hear their complaints about the school, and how she came to understand from research and experience the frustration some teachers felt in their poor communication with their students.

Many teachers and administrators felt they were "not asking the right questions" of either the children or their own teaching strategies, and I was asked to help them find ways of helping themselves. As an aide, tutor, traveling librarian, and "visiting fireman" occasionally asked to talk about archaeology or show slides of other countries in which I had done fieldwork, I served numerous functions in classrooms across a wide range of grade levels and subject areas for five years. I participated and observed, shared data, and acted as change agent at the request of the institution's members. During this period, some of the teachers enrolled in graduate courses of study which included some anthropology and linguistics courses I taught. They then used techniques of ethnographic fieldwork and data interpretation in their own classes and schools and incorporated into their teaching some of the observation skills associated with anthropology. Some teachers collected data on their own practices in guiding language learning for their preschool children at home; others agreed to allow me to participate and observe in their homes, recording use of language and language input for their children. Particularly critical to these teachers' understanding and acceptance of ethnography in familiar educational settings—both their classrooms and their homes— was their view that the ethnographic/linguistic research was in response to their felt needs, and they were themselves involved.

The sections above focussed on questions 1 and 2, relating to design and data collection. Further, her sources of data have been presented: the parents, the school, as well as the children. In the next section, questions related to general levels of observation will be explored using additional aspects of Heath's ethnography.

> *What guideline questions does this portion of the report answer?*
> *What did you learn about Heath's sources and methods of data collection?*
> *What additional information did you learn about the frameworks used for data gathering within the context?*

Heath proceeds to review the use of questions by children's caretakers and concludes that the kinds and uses of questions children become socialized to expect are dependent on the network of people who ask those questions. She then goes on to report classroom teachers' use of questions with their own children.

Classroom Teachers and Their Own Children

Within their homes, children of the classroom teachers involved in this study were socialized into a fairly small network of language users: mother, father, siblings, and maids or grandparents. Children below the age of four rarely communicated with anyone on an extended basis except these primary associates. Visits to Sunday School, the grocery store, shopping centers, and so on provided very limited opportunities for questions addressed to the children by nonintimates. Within the homes, talk to preschool children emphasized questions. In their questioning routines with preverbal as well as verbal children, adults supplied the entire context, giving questions and answering them (cf. Gleason 1973) or giving questions and then pausing to hold conversational space for a hypothetical answer before moving on to the next statement, which assumed information from the hypothetical answer (cf. Snow 1977).

MOTHER (addressing an 8-week-old infant): *You want your teddy bear?*

MOTHER: *Yes, you want your bear.*

. . .

MOTHER (addressing her 2-month-old infant): *You don't know what to make of those lights, do you?*

Pause (3 seconds)

MOTHER: *That's right. I know you don't like them. Let's move over here.* (picks up infant and moves away from lights)

. . .

MOTHER (addressing her child age 2;9): *Didja forget your coat?*

MOTHER: *Yes, you did. Let's go back 'n get it.*

When parents wanted to teach a politeness formula, such as thank you or please, they used interrogatives: "Can you say 'thank you'?" "What do you say?" (cf. Gleason and Weintraub 1976). Questions served a wide variety of functions in adult-child interactions. They allowed adults to hold pseudo-conversations with children, to direct their attention to specific events or objects in the array of stimuli about them, and to link formulaic responses to appropriate occasions. Perhaps most important, adults' use of questions trained children to act as question-answerers, as experts on knowledge about the world, especially the names and attributes of items in their environment and those introduced to them through books.

> *What types of recurrent interactions are described?*
> *What are the goals of the interactions?*
> *What products of the interactions are described?*
> *From what point(s) of view?*

Recurrent parent-child interactions are described, with stress on the questioning activities in the teachers' homes. Heath suggests that the verbal interactions between the teachers and their children are adult-guided and serve to place the child in the role of question-answerer about world knowledge. She goes on to describe adult-child verbal interactions that took place with grandparents and older siblings as with the parents (teachers). This was done to elaborate her model or understanding of observed patterns. Her summary follows.

> In summary, teachers socializing their own preschoolers to language depended heavily on questions. They used questions to teach their children what they should attend to when looking at a book ("What's that?" "Where's the puppy?" "What does he have in his hand?"). The children were taught to label (Ninio and Bruner 1978), to search out pieces of pictures, to name parts of the whole, and to talk about these out of context. As the children grew older, adults used questions to add power to their directives ("Stop that! Did you hear me?") and to call particular attention to the infraction committed ("Put that back. Don't you know that's not yours?"). Adults saw questions as necessary to train children, to cause them to respond verbally, and to be trained as conversational partners.

> *What does this reveal about the products of the interactions that*
> *had not been stated before?*
> *From whose point of view?*

Here, Heath explains the instructional value of the questioning interaction from the child's perspective as seen from the adults' vantage point. After summarizing her description of questions in teachers' homes, Heath introduces the reader to the Trackton community. Although many ethnographies describe only one culture or context, Heath's study is comparative (a comparison among Trackton home questions, teachers' home questions, and the questions asked in school); therefore, contrasting data must be gathered and analyzed. This contrast can be seen in the next excerpt, which contrasts the one above.

That was not the case for children in Trackton, as examination of the role of questions in their language socialization indicates. Questions addressed by adults to children occurred far less frequently in Trackton than in the homes of teachers. In Trackton, adults were not observed playing peek-a-boo games with young children; thus, a major source of Q-I questions was eliminated. Adults and siblings also did not direct questions to preverbal infants; instead, they made statements about them to someone else which conveyed the same information as questions directed by teachers to their children. Trackton adults would say of a crying preverbal infant: "Sump'n's the matter with that child." The equivalent in the teacher's home would be to direct a question or series of questions to the child: "What's the matter?" "Does something hurt you?" "Are you hungry?" Trackton adults did not attempt to engage children as conversational partners until they were seen as realistic sources of information and competent partners in talk.

It has been suggested that the language used by adults, especially mothers, in speaking to young children has numerous special properties; some of these develop because of the limited range of topics which can be discussed with young children (Shatz and Gelman 1977). In addition, most of the research on mother-child interaction has been done in homes where a single child and a single parent were recorded in their interactions (Brown 1973). In this situation, mothers have no one other than their children to talk or be with, and language interactions with their children may thus be intensified over those which would occur if other conversational partners were consistently present. In Trackton, adults almost always had someone else around to talk to; rarely were mothers or other adults left alone in the home with young children (cf. Young 1970, Ward 1971, Stack 1976).

What interaction patterns have been described?
What goals of the interactions have been described?

Unlike the interactions in the teachers' homes, those in the students' homes were more closed—more telling than asking. To this point, Heath has provided a general frame and contrast among the groups. In the next section of her report, she describes the products of the parent-child interactions more fully.

> In Trackton, children did not hold high positions as information-givers or question-answerers, especially in response to questions for which adults already knew the answer. When children were asked questions, they were primarily of five types. Table [5–1] provides a description of the types of questions used with preschoolers in Trackton. The various uses noted here do not include all those evidenced in Trackton, but they constitute the major types used by adults to young children. Crucial to the flexibility in the uses of interrogative forms is their embeddedness in particular

Table 5–1
Types of questions asked of children in Trackton

Types	Responses Called For	Examples
Analogy	Nonspecific comparison of one item, event, or person with another	What's that like? (referring to a flat tire on a neighbor's car) Doug's car, never fixed.
Story-starter	Question asking for explanation of events leading to first questioner's question	Question 1: Did you see Maggie's dog yesterday? Question 2: What happened to Maggie's dog?
Accusatory	Either nonverbal response and a lowered head or a story creative enough to take the questioner's attention away from the original infraction	What's that all over your face? Do you know 'bout that big mud-puddle . . .
A-I	Specific information known to addressee, but not to questioner	What do you want? Juice.
Q-I	Specific piece of information known to both questioner and addressee	What's your name, huh? Teeg.

Source: Heath 1982, from *Doing the Ethnography of Schooling*, ed. by George Spindler. Copyright © 1982 by CBS College Publishing. Reprinted with permission of Holt, Rinehart and Winston, CBS College Publishing.

communication and interpersonal contexts. In the analysis of types, it should be evident that there is a distinction between what some of these interrogatives mean and what the speaker means in uttering them.

> *Have the products of the interactions been described from one or more points of view?*
> *Has the developing model been presented?*
> *What is it?*

Here, the products of the interactions have been described from the points of view of both parent and child, using examples of their dialogue to illustrate her model of interaction. After providing further examples of questioning language and the uses of questions in the Trackton homes, Heath draws her conclusions.

> In summary, children in Trackton were not viewed as information-givers in their interactions with adults, nor were they considered appropriate conversation partners, and thus they did not learn to act as such. They were not excluded from language participation; their linguistic environment was rich with a variety of styles, speakers, and topics. Language input was, however, not especially constructed for them; in particular, they were not engaged as conversationalists through special types of questions addressed to them.

> *What further information does the summary reveal about the interactions?*

From the child's point of view, Heath explains what nonsocialization into the give-and-take conversation form means. She then goes on to describe the kinds of questions and their uses in the classroom.

> Questioning in the classrooms by teachers involved in the study reported here fit the general patterns revealed in research in other classrooms. Questions dominated classroom talk; the predominant type of question used in classroom lessons called for feedback of information included in the lesson; questions which asked for analysis, synthesis, or evaluation of lesson data occurred much less frequently and were used predominantly with top-level reading groups. Of particular importance in this study is attention to types of questions used in the classroom as compared with the homes of teachers and students.

In lessons, teachers often asked questions which required confirmation of certain skills necessary to exhibit knowledge. Attention to appropriate stimuli—the person reading, a letter chart, or a specific page of a book—was tested by questions. Teachers used these in extended interactions with single students, small groups, and the entire class. If directed to a specific student, this question type demanded a response, either by display of the skill or by verbal confirmation. If directed to a group of students or the class, these questions were not to be answered, for they were merely forerunners to questions which would require answers.

What are the goals of these interactions?
Do they tell anything about group membership?

We see that goals of school interactions require children to be somewhat facile conversationalists. They need to engage in question-answering behavior—behavior we have been told the children had not been socialized to perform. Uses of language in the Trackton homes contrast in specific ways with the use of questions in the classroom.

The learning of language uses in Trackton had not prepared children to cope with three major characteristics of the many questions used in classrooms. First, they had not learned how to respond to utterances which were interrogative in form, but directive in pragmatic function (e.g., "Why don't you use the one on the back shelf?" = "Get the one on the back shelf"). Second, Q-I questions which expected students to feed back information already known to the teacher were outside the general experience of Trackton students. Third, they had little or no experience with questions which asked for display of specific skills and content information acquired primarily from a familiarity with books and ways of talking about books (e.g., "Can you find Tim's name?" "Who will come help Tim find his way home?"). In short, school questions were unfamiliar in their frequency, purposes, and types, and in the domains of content knowledge and skills display they assumed on the part of students.

From what point of view is the comparison made?

Heath concludes her chapter with a section called "Intervention: A Two-Way Path." This serves to suggest solutions, as well as stimulate the reader to think about the implications of the findings for classroom practice.

> *Intervention: A Two-Way Path*
>
> The task of schools is to transmit certain kinds of content and skills, but much of this transmission depends on classroom questions. For Trackton students to succeed academically, therefore, they had to learn to use questions according to the rules of classroom usage. However, intervention did not have to be one-way; teachers could also learn about the rules for community uses of questions. The choice in intervention was, therefore, not only to change Trackton students, but also to provide an opportunity for alterations in teachers' behaviors and knowledge. . . .

Heath's paper is comprehensive and clear. The only item that is not directly described but must be inferred or interpolated by the reader deals with elaboration of the specific ethnographic methods used and the kinds and extent of the regrounding procedures. We know that Heath gathered voluminous data in a variety of contexts, provided a good deal of feedback to the Trackton teachers, and suggested alternative instructional dialogue, as well. But, from her descriptions of language use in Trackton homes, in teachers' homes, and in the classroom, we can only assume that case studies were carried out similarly across settings and that extensive regrounding was carried out over time. Unfortunately, this particular kind of information is sometimes omitted from ethnographic reports when inclusion would be helpful, particularly for the reader who is less familiar with ethnographic methodology.

A SAMPLING OF RESULTS

Ethnographic studies have provided rich information about verbal and nonverbal interactions within and across classrooms, as well as between classrooms and communities. Green and Wallat (1981) have mapped instructional conversations within school lessons in order to identify variables that affect communication and learning. They have shown that many social rules are adhered to throughout a lesson. For successful instructional interaction to occur, students must interpret the broad range of verbal and nonverbal signals sent by the teacher and by other students. Erickson and his colleagues (Florio 1978; Erickson and Schultz 1981; Florio and Schultz 1979; Erickson 1976, 1977) have found that during a typical class session, students move through different types of participant structures, or contexts. Some structures have established names, such as "show-and-tell," while others do not. However, each participant structure requires a somewhat different mode of cooperation and learning and calls for different rules for evaluating how to behave. Students must learn access strategies before engaging in the activity; knowing how to do this becomes a precondition for learning.

McDermott (1978) studied nonverbal behavior to investigate the cultural context of learning to read in an urban elementary school. He showed that when students were divided into high and low groups, teacher time with the low group was taken up with such control behavior as looking around the room to ward off possible interruptions. As a result, children in the low group received less actual reading instruction and did less substantive work than children in the high reading group. This management behavior, he found, emanated from the teacher's belief that students in the low achievement group required more explicit and constant direction than their higher achieving classmates.

Gumperz, Simons, and Cook-Gumperz (1982) conducted a school-home ethnographic study in which first- and fourth-grade classrooms were observed by a participant observer, and class sessions were tape recorded. Collins (1982), in a research paper based on the same project, reported that teachers tended to ask word level and decoding questions of the low group, while students in the high group were asked questions dealing with text content. In particular, the pitch and intonation of the poor readers appeared to elicit more word level and phonic questions from the teachers. Their results suggest that the poor readers received different instruction than the good readers, with less instructional time focussing on thinking and reasoning about the content of what they read.

Heath (1980) conducted a comparative study of two cultural groups with distinctly different oral traditions whose children attended the same school. The first group was quite literal in its use of language, while the other was expansive and fanciful. Although children in both groups tended to have difficulty in school, the first group of youngsters was more successful in the initial stages of each of the early grades, while the second group's elaborated responses to the teachers' "wh" questions were treated as digressions. Heath describes how each oral tradition is rich in its own way but uniquely at variance with school language and teacher expectations.

Au (1980) studied reading lessons in the Hawaiian Kamehameha (KEEP) Schools to identify the participant structures. During reading comprehension time, she found recurring "talk-story"—a cooperative speech event that was a function of friendly Hawaiian dialogue. When the reading lessons functioned as talk-stories, they were usually more successful. However, most lessons were not planned with this communication model in mind. This and other studies (Au and Jordan 1981) have indicated that although children may come to school with communicative conventions not shared by their teachers, classroom interaction patterns can be changed to encompass these conventions. And when this is done, learning can be facilitated. Results of these and other ethnographic studies (listed below) help researchers and practitioners understand the communicative interactions that affect the way children behave and learn.

IN SUMMARY

Ethnographic research describes interrelationships as they typically occur on a day-to-day basis. Educational ethnography examines the educational culture—the social interactions and behaviors that affect ways in which instruction is carried out and children learn. Because the focus is on human behavior from the learner's point of view, ethnographers often immerse themselves as participant observers in the cultures they study. Recurring patterns of behavior are used to formulate hypotheses that are validated by regrounding with other persons or the same persons in other similar situations.

To read an ethnography, it is helpful to look for information regarding the culture being studied, the means by which it was studied, the recurring patterns of interaction that were identified, and the ways in which all of these were validated.

REFERENCES

Au, K. H. (1980). Participation structures in a reading lesson with Hawaiian children: Analysis of a culturally appropriate instructional event. *Anthropology and Education Quarterly, 11*, 91–115.

Au, K., & Jordan, C. (1981). Teaching reading to Hawaiian children. In H. Trueba, G. P. Guthrie, & K. Au (Eds.), *Culture and the bilingual classroom: Studies in classroom ethnography.* Rowley, MA: Newbury House.

Bronfenbrenner, U. (1976). The experimental ecology of education. *Educational Researcher, 5*, 5–15.

Collins, J. (1982). Differential treatment in reading instruction. Paper on final report of School-home Ethnography Project. National Institute of Education No. G-78-0082.

Comte, A. (1973). *Systems of positive policy* (Rev. ed.). New York: B. Franklin. (Original work published in 1875.)

Durkheim, E. (1956). *Education and sociology.* Glencoe, IL: The Free Press.

Erickson, F. (1976). Gatekeeping encounters: A social selection process. In P. R. Sanday (Ed.), *Anthropology and the public interest.* New York: Academic Press.

Erickson, F. (1977). Some approaches to inquiry in school-community ethnography. *Anthropology and Education Quarterly, 8*, 58–69.

Erickson, F., & Schultz, J. (1981). When is a context? Some issues and methods in the analysis of social competence. In J. Green & C. Wallat (Eds.), *Ethnography and language in educational settings.* Norwood, NJ: Ablex.

Florio S. (1978). Learning how to go to school. Doctoral dissertation, Harvard University.

Florio, S., & Schultz, J. (1979). Social competence at home and at school. *Theory into Practice, 18*(4), 234–243.

Green, J. L., & Wallat, C. (1981). Mapping instructional conversations—a sociolinguistic ethnography. In J. L. Green & C. Wallat (Eds.), *Ethnography and language in educational settings.* Norwood, NJ: Ablex.

Gumperz, J., Simons, H., & Cook-Gumperz, J. (1982). Final Report on School-Home Ethnography Project. National Institute of Education (No. G-78-0082).

Heath, S. B. (1980, November). *What no bedtime story means: Narrative skills at home and school.* Paper presented at Terman Conference, Stanford University.

Heath, S. B. (1982). Questioning at home and at school: A comparative study. In G. Spindler (Ed.), *Doing the ethnography of schooling.* New York: Holt, Rinehart and Winston.

Heath, S. B. (1983). *Way with words: Ethnography of communication, communities, and classrooms.* New York: Cambridge University Press.

Husserl, E. (1931). *Ideas: General introduction to pure phenomenology.* New York: Macmillan.

Malinowski, B. (1922). *The argonauts of the western Pacific.* London: Routledge and Kegan Paul.

McDermott, R. (1978). Relating and learning: An analysis of two classroom reading groups. In R. Shiney (Ed.), *Linguistics and reading.* Rowley, MA: Newbury House.

Ogbu, J. (1978). *Minority education and caste: The American system in cross cultural perspective.* San Francisco: Academic Press.

Philips, S. (1972). Participant structures and communicative competence: Warm Springs children in community and classroom. In C. Cazden, V. P. John & D. Hymes (Eds.), *Functions of language in the classroom.* New York: Teachers College Press.

Schultz, J., & Florio, S. (1979). Stop and freeze: The negotiation of social and physical space in a kindergarten/first grade classroom. *Anthropology and Education Quarterly, 10*(3), 166–181.

Schutz, A. (1970). *On phenomenological and social relations.* Chicago: University of Chicago Press.

Scollon, R. & Scollon, S. B. K. (1981). *Narrative, literacy, and face in interethnic communication.* Norwood, NJ: Ablex.

Spindler, G. (Ed.). (1982). *Doing the ethnography of schooling.* New York: CBS College Publishing.

Weber, M. (1947). *The theory of social and economic organization.* New York: Oxford University Press.

ADDITIONAL SOURCES
OF ETHNOGRAPHIC METHODOLOGIES

Gilmore, P., & Glatthorn, A. A. (1982). *Ethnography and education: Children in and out of school.* Philadelphia: University of Pennsylvania Press.

Green, J. & Wallat, C. (Eds.). (1981). *Ethnography and language in educational settings.* Norwood, NJ: Ablex.

Guba, E. G. (1978). *Toward a methodology of naturalistic inquiry in educational evaluation.* Los Angeles: Center for the Study of Evaluation, UCLA Graduate School of Education.

Kaplan, A. (1984). *The conduct of inquiry: Methodology for the behavioral sciences.* New York: Harper and Row.

Kaplan, M., Galbreath, D., & Vargas, C. (Eds.). (1980). *Ethnographic and qualitative methods in educational research: A selected annotated bibliography.* Charlottesville: University of Virginia, School of Education.

Rist, R. C. (1977). On the relations among educational research paradigms: From disdain to detente. *Anthropology and Education, 8* [Special issue, "Exploring Qualitative and Quantitative Research Methodologies in Education"].

Spindler, G. D. (1963). The character structure of anthropology. In G. Spindler (Ed.), *Education and culture.* New York: Holt, Rinehart and Winston.

Spradley, J. P. (1980). *Participant observation.* New York: Holt, Rinehart and Winston.

ADDITIONAL EXAMPLES
OF ETHNOGRAPHIC STUDIES

Florio, S. (1979). The problem of dead letters: Social perspectives on the teaching of writing. *The Elementary School Journal, 80,* 1–7.

Goffman, E. (1961). *Encounters: Two studies in the sociology of interaction.* New York: Bobbs-Merrill.

Gumperz, J. J. (1975). The conversational analysis of social meaning: A study of classroom interaction. In M. Sanches & B. Blount (Eds.), *Sociocultural Dimensions of Language Use.* New York: Academy Press.

Hickman, J. (1981, December). New perspective on response to literature: Research in an elementary school setting. *Research on the Teaching of English, 15*(4), 343–354.

Leacock, E. B. (1969). *Teaching and learning in city schools.* New York: Basic Books.

Mehan, H. (1969). *Learning lessons: Social organization in the classroom.* Cambridge, MA: Harvard University Press.

Michaels, S. & Cook-Gumperz, J. (1979). A study of sharing time with first grade students: Discourse narratives in the classroom. In *Proceedings of the Berkeley Linguistic Society* (Vol. 5, pp. 649–659).

Schiefflen, B. B. (1979). Getting it together: An ethnographic approach to the study of the development of communicative competence. In E. Ochs and B. B. Schiefflen (Eds.), *Developmental pragmatics.* New York: Academic Press.

Watson-Gegeo, K. & Boggs, S. (1977). From verbal play to talk story: The role of routines in speech events among Hawaiian children. In S. Ervin-Tripp & C. Mitchell-Kernan (Eds.), *Child discourse.* New York: Academic Press.

Wilkenson, L. C. & Calculator, S. (1982, Spring). Request and responses in peer directed reading groups. *American Educational Research Journal, 19*(1), 107–120.

Chapter 6

The Logic
of Experimental Research:
Simple Designs

In this chapter, we will deal with research that establishes a cause-and-effect relationship between a single educational variable and its outcome. To do this, researchers use what is called the *scientific method*. The goal of this type of research is to specify conditions under which specific results can be obtained. We will examine this approach for simple situations in this chapter, before turning to more complex situations in the next.

THE LOGIC
OF EXPERIMENTAL RESEARCH

The logic of the experimental approach is straightforward. In the simplest cases, researchers *control* a situation and *manipulate* only one variable. The results of the manipulation are then observed. If the researcher has controlled the situation so that only one variable has changed, then the observed results can be attributed to those manipulations. In these simple cases, a researcher would compare two situations: one in which nothing was done, and one in which the manipulated variable was introduced.

For example, if we were interested in whether sentence combining improved writing, we might do a simple experiment. Using two groups of students equivalent in all relevant respects, we would give one group instruction in sentence combining. The other group would receive no such instruction. If the two groups were truly equivalent prior to the instruction, any differences in writing at the end of the experiment could be attributed to the effect of the instruction.

There are dangers here. In order to make a valid statement of cause and effect on the basis of experimental results, *all* conditions (other than the manipulated variable) must be *exactly* identical for the two groups. In order to ensure this, researchers use a rigorous set of procedures. We will first detail the steps in the scientific method and then examine the procedures of experimental research: hypothesis testing, experimental control, research designs, and statistical analyses.

Some research appears to be experimental, having two groups with one characteristic differing between them. A common example of this involves good versus poor readers. Many studies find two groups of readers—one good and one poor—and measure some performance characteristic. Since the researcher *measured* rather than *manipulated* the reading abilities, any number of other factors that were not measured could have contributed to the results. These situations, in which the variables are not manipulated, are sometimes called *quasi experiments*. True statements of causality cannot be made on the basis of quasi experiments, although other sorts of conclusions are possible. (A discussion of these types of studies is included in chapter 8.)

The Scientific Method

A basic assumption of all experimental research is that phenomena can be directly observed, measured, or at least inferred from direct sensory observations. Mathematics and logic can be used, but almost everything else is excluded. The goal of this scientific method is to be able to *explain* why some event occurred. That is, one should be able to specify the conditions under which an event will or will not occur.

A researcher usually begins with a *hypothesis* that is a first approximation of that explanation. Then, with that hypothesis in mind, the researcher sets up situations in which relevant variables can be manipulated to see if the hypothesis is valid. In this case, the question is whether the hypothesis accounts for the observations.

Two possibilities arise. One is that the researcher conducts an experiment that produces results contrary to those predicted by the hypothesis. If this happens, the researcher adds the new data to the old body of data and formulates a new hypothesis that does account for all of the data. The whole process is continued until the experiment produces results that are consistent with the hypothesis.

The second possibility is that the results of the experiment are consistent with the hypothesis. At first appearance, this might seem to be the end of the process. However, normal conditions require that a *replication* be performed; the same experiment should be repeated. To be a true replication, the conditions must be the same as those in the original experiment. (This is one reason for the elaborate detail of research reports—other researchers can then *replicate* the experiment.) A replication helps guarantee that the results were not due to unknown or unusual factors in a single experiment.

If results could be replicated *whenever* the experimental conditions are fulfilled, we would have ultimate confidence in the results. However, an experiment can never be replicated *exactly*. Even though a researcher tries to set up the same conditions as in an original experiment, many elements will be different. For example, the same participants should not be used in a replication, or the initial experiences of the participants would be different in the replication.

Most often, replications introduce changes into the original procedures. Different participants, different values for the variables, and often different materials are used. These differences increase the generalizability of the results, demonstrating that they can be obtained under many different conditions. (This issue will be discussed further in chapter 9.)

The scientific method requires that the researcher develop new tests of the hypothesis. Figure 6–1 shows a flow chart illustrating this process.

Figure 6–1 reveals a strange situation: There seems to be no way out of the loop. In a strict sense, this is exactly what the scientific method suggests. A researcher never proves a hypothesis conclusively. When a given hypothesis has been experimentally tested on a number of occasions

Figure 6–1
Flow chart for the scientific method

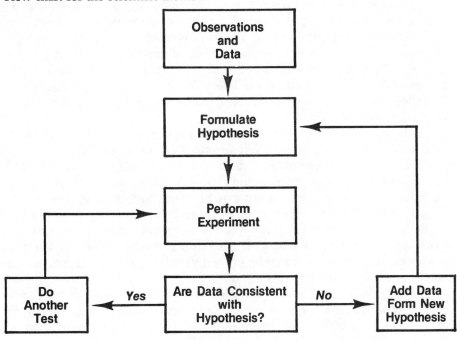

and is found to be consistent with the results, it can be believed with confidence. However, hypotheses are rejected if they are not consistent with the data.

Another caution is in order: Scientific methodology assumes that experiments are done properly and precisely. Results (data) can be used to reject hypotheses if we are certain they have been obtained without flaws. If an experiment is faulty, the data produced should not be used to make decisions about hypotheses.

Therefore, experiments must be rigorously scrutinized for procedural or other flaws. When flaws are uncovered, new experiments must be performed. The process of critical analysis characterizes the scientific method. Knowledge is assumed to be cumulative; each new piece is added to the rest. However, knowledge should be public; it should always be subject to reevaluation and further testing or experimentation.

Definitions and Variables

Because there is such emphasis on precision, everything in an experiment must be specified. This includes the definitions of the variables of interest. Moreover, these definitions have to match the assumptions of the experimental method; they must specify variables in terms of what can be observed, measured, or calculated.

One version of these definitions is sometimes called an *operational definition*. An operational definition describes the processes one must use to observe what is being defined. For example, *achievement* can be defined as the score on a specific test, or quality of writing can be defined in terms of length of sentences or *T*-units. The definition must be clear and unambiguous. Any disagreement should be settled by performing experiments with different definitions. The value of using these definitions is that they are precise. Anyone can use the definitions in the same way the original researcher did.

Three kinds of variables are used in experiments: *independent, dependent*, and *extraneous*. Independent variables are those that the researcher manipulates. In instructional studies, a common independent variable is the type of instruction given to the students. Often one method is tested against another. The independent variable is the method; it assumes *values*, which are, in this case, specific methods of instruction. Another example is the type of question a student is asked by a teacher. If one group of students is asked text-based questions and the other is asked script- or reader-based questions, the independent variable is question type, and the values are text-based and reader-based.

Dependent variables are those measured or observed in the experimental situation. We measure performance and assume it depends on the manipulated variable. The dependent variable must be specified in the same way the independent variable is. There are also many choices. For instance, if we are measuring quality of writing, we might measure *T*-units, sentence length, semantic complexity, or total composition length. The definitional criteria apply here as well: If someone disagrees, he or she can resolve the disagreement by using another dependent variable in a new experiment.

Extraneous variables include all the other variables that can be present in an experimental situation, such as the temperature, time of day, and so on. In instructional research, we assume that these variables do not have a significant effect on the dependent variable. However, not all extraneous variables are so harmless. Some do have major effects on the experimental results.

The problem in interpreting data that are not the direct result of the experimental manipulations was mentioned above. Namely, extraneous variables can affect the results in ways that the researcher cannot easily detect. Because of this problem, a great deal of effort in experimental research goes into *controlling* extraneous variables.

Experimental Control

Conceptually, one of the simplest methods of controlling extraneous variables is *eliminating* or *isolating* them. For example, an experiment might take place in a single classroom, rather than in different environments. This isolates the students from the many extraneous variables outside the classroom. (However, a large—perhaps infinite—number of extraneous variables still exists in the classroom.) Since most instructional experiments are extended over time, it is not possible to isolate students effectively from all extraneous variables.

Another technique of control is that of *balancing* or *counterbalancing*. In this method, those extraneous variables known to have effects on the experimental treatments (independent variables) are identified, and they are distributed equally over the groups in the experiment. For example, students in an experimental study may be required to write summaries of passages. The order in which students read the passages and complete the summaries may have some effect on the quality of the summaries. To prevent this, the order of the passages may be counterbalanced: Each passage would occur first for some students and last for others. When the average performance is examined for all students, an equal number will have had to deal with each passage in each serial position.

As with all choices, there are benefits and costs. In counterbalancing, the assumption is that the effects of the extraneous variables can be equally distributed across the groups of students in the experiment. It is not always possible to distribute the effects equally in practice, but counterbalancing is better than allowing the effects of the extraneous variables to go uncontrolled.

The final method of control, *randomization*, assumes that not all extraneous variables can be identified. Any unknown variables will balance themselves out if they are allowed to affect the experiments in a *random* fashion. This means that the experimenter should assign variables to groups randomly. In the example used earlier, the passages to be summarized could be given to each student in a random order. If there is a large enough number of students, the random orders should assign each passage to each position equally.

Grouping Subjects

This is a specific case of the general problem of experimental control. When we interpret the results of an experiment, we assume that everything except the manipulated conditions was constant or equal. That is also true of the groups from populations we choose to study. If we used two methods of teaching, using one with each of two different groups, we might want to compare the performances of the groups at the end of the study. If one group performed better, we might attribute it to the method. However, suppose we had accidentally chosen two groups that differed in ability. We would not be able to distinguish the effects of ability of the students from the effects of the teaching method. These two variables are said to be *confounded*.

To prevent experimental results from being contaminated by confounded variables, researchers use a variety of experimental control techniques. Assignment of students to various groups is a particularly troublesome problem for experimental research in instructional problems. Since most students are already assigned to classes, researchers often are faced with the problem of having to give one class one instructional treatment and another class a completely different treatment.

When researchers have to deal with classes, they often randomly assign more than one class to a treatment to replicate that part of the experiment. This minimizes the chance that a single class of different ability will affect the results of the study. When the conditions under which the research is conducted do not require that the students be kept in classes, researchers can form groups by randomly assigning each student to one of the groups. Again, this minimizes the possibility that any group will be composed of unusual or unrepresentative students.

The population that a researcher chooses is important to the conclusions drawn at the end of the study. It is also closely related to the problem being studied. For example, it would be a waste of time to research advanced study skills with nonreaders. In a study of the effects of phonics instruction on reading achievement, different conclusions would be reached for different population groups, say comparing prereaders to highly literate adults.

The population choice a researcher makes must be carefully described and rationalized by the theory, problem, and purpose of the experiment. Ultimately, this choice will determine the generalizability of the results obtained from the experiment, all else being equal.

Design of Experiments

In this chapter, we are going to deal with one simple design. In the next chapter, we will consider what happens when experiments use more complex designs.

We have been describing situations that, in general, assume experimental research can be done by selecting two values of an independent variable, administering one value to each of two groups and measuring the results. This is a simple *two-group design*.

The major problem with this sort of experiment is that the real world is not so simple: More than two factors usually contribute to any given result. You can probably list many factors that would influence reading or writing performance. As we discussed earlier, to be ecologically valid, an experiment must represent the real world (Bronfenbrenner 1976). Thus, there are special difficulties in interpreting two-group experiments.

Researchers can overcome this problem by using more independent variables in a more complex design. Such designs will be described in the next chapter.

Control Groups

In an experiment, a *control group* is one in which the subjects are not given any treatment; they are left alone, under the same conditions (except for the manipulation of the independent variable) as the experimental group. This is done so that the data collected in the experiment will allow us to compare the treatment conditions to normal conditions. This is particularly important in educational research, since we would not want to adopt a new method of teaching or evaluating unless we were reasonably certain that it was better than what we were already using.

Theoretically, the control group is identical to the other group (or groups, in more complex designs) in the experiment, except for the experimental treatment given. This use of a control group allows us to assess the magnitude of the effects of the independent variable. It also allows us to attribute the experimental effects directly to the independent variable, not to some confounding extraneous variable. For example, students may often react differently when they know they are being observed. (Try visiting a new classroom and watch how frequently the students observe *you!*) The use of a control group enables us to feel confident that *both* groups of subjects were reacting to being observed.

Statistical Analysis

Since an experimental situation is so rigorously controlled, we usually have a great deal of confidence in the data we collect. However, we can only use a *sample* of subjects in any experiment. We must then analyze our data to know whether the sample we have used is representative of the entire population.

The data collected in experiments can be analyzed in a number of different ways. We have already encountered many of them. A popular view, however, associates experiments with numbers. This involves the use of *statistics*.

Statistical procedures assign a probability value to the data we collect. Remember, probabilities range from 0.0 to 1.0. A value of 0.0 means that the event will *not* occur, while a value of 1.0 means that it *must* occur. The higher the values (closer to 1.0), the more likely the event will occur.

For the simple experimental situations we have discussed, the data are often analyzed by using a procedure called a *t*-test. This is a statistical procedure that tells us how likely we would be to obtain a difference between the means of the two groups by chance. If there is a large probability that the differences could have occurred by chance, we are unwilling to feel confident about any differences we have measured. But if the probability is small, we are willing to believe that the differences are meaningful. *Large* and *small* are relative terms and can, within limits, be set by the experimenter.

Hypothesis Testing

To make all this clear, the research sets up a hypothesis to test. For the two-group situations we have been describing, the hypothesis is often based on the difference between the means of the two groups. The technical term for this is the *null hypothesis*. The theory is that there will be no difference between the means of the population from which the groups were sampled. Compare this to the scientific method—we never prove something *is* true, we only prove it *is not* true.

When the statistical test shows that the differences are likely to be by chance, we have to *accept* the null hypothesis. When the probabilities are small, we *reject* the null hypothesis.

Every null hypothesis has an *alternate hypothesis*. When we have two samples, the null hypothesis takes the form $H_0: \mu_1 = \mu_2$. The symbol μ is used to represent the mean of the populations being studied. Statistics deal with samples, so we do not usually know what the population values are. But statistical tests allow inferences about how closely the sample means (represented by the symbol $\bar{X}$) approximate the population means.

There is also an *alternative hypothesis*, which is set up to account for the other possibility, $H_1: \mu_1 \neq \mu_2$. If we reject the null hypothesis, which states there is no difference, we are obligated to accept the alternative hypothesis, which states there *is* a difference.

We can never be absolutely certain of our decisions. The probability associated with the statistical test determines how confident we should be. Conventionally, researchers have adopted a criterion that results should have probabilities of occurring by chance less than 0.05 ($p < 0.05$), or 5 out of 100 times. To be even more certain, some researchers set their criterion more conservatively, using 0.01 or even 0.001.

The other element that allows more confidence is the number of subjects used in each experiment. This is reflected by the *degrees of freedom* (df). The larger the df, the more confidence we can have in the results. Larger values for df indicate the statistical tests will detect differences among the treatments. For the *t*-test, the df are reported in the following way:

$$t (28) = 3.14, p < .05 .$$

This indicates there were 30 subjects in the experiment, and the difference between the means of the two groups would occur by chance fewer than 5 times out of 100. The *t*-test always has fewer degrees of freedom than subjects. For statistical reasons, 1 df is lost for every population estimate made. In *t*-tests, we estimate the population mean for each, losing 2 df.

Interpreting the Results

Once the researcher has analyzed the results statistically, he then has to interpret them. The task is to place the results in a context that relates to other work, theory, or practice (or all three). Researchers tend to overstate the relevance of a particular finding. We have to guard against generalizing the findings beyond the experimental conditions, which includes staying within the limits of the characteristics of the populations used in the study.

Two sorts of validity must be considered in interpreting the results of an experiment. The first is called *internal* validity. For an experiment to be internally valid, the experimental treatment must have made a difference. This should be very clear. If there are no significant differences in the experiment, there is no way to interpret those findings.

The second concept is *external* validity; it refers to how the experimental results relate to the real world. For example, is the population appropriate for the desired interpretation? Or were the settings in which the data were collected unusual or nonrepresentative? A more complete discussion of these issues is found in Campbell and Stanley (1966).

A final caution about validity: Often a researcher finds results that are statistically significant but cannot be easily translated into educational practice. Unless there is a demonstrable use for the results, beware of researchers who jump from their data to practice. At the least, the researcher should verify results in educational settings before making recommendations for practice. This guarantees that the results will be educationally and statistically significant.

QUESTIONS FOR AN EXPERIMENT

As you read a report of experimental research, ask specific questions. You should be able to answer these questions precisely.

1. What is the problem being studied? What is the hypothesis? (State it/them.)
2. Is this study related to other work and theory on the same problem? (State how.)
3. What are the independent and dependent variables? (Name them.)
4. Was the independent variable actually manipulated? (State how.)
5. What were the characteristics of the subject population that was used? (Identify them.)
6. What was the design of the experiment? (Describe it.)
7. How were the data analyzed? (Name the procedure.)
8. Were the results statistically significant? (Indicate which ones.)
9. Are the results contaminated by confounded variables? (State how.)
10. Are the results educationally or psychologically significant? (State why.)
11. Are the results related back to theory or prior work? (Specify how.)
12. Are the implications limited to the conditions of the experiment? (Summarize them.)

An Example

Christopherson (1978) was interested in the effects of teaching students semantic roles on recall of written prose. He sets the background for the experiment:

> *What is the problem being studied?*
> *What is the hypothesis?*
> *Is the study related to other work and theory on the same problem?*

The linguistic and psychological importance of semantic roles, such as Agent and Instrument, has been the object of much study in recent years. Many linguists have found semantic roles to be useful in describing the structure and content of language. Initially, most of this work focused on roles within individual sentences (e.g., Chafe, 1979; Fillmore, 1968; Fries, 1952; Halliday, 1967; Longacre, 1964; Weinreich, 1963). Fillmore (1968), the most prominent of these linguists, described several semantic roles which are found in sentences: Agentive, Objective, Instrumental, Locative, Dative, and Factitive. Fillmore's work not only contributed directly to an understanding of the importance of semantic roles in language, but also contributed indirectly through the linguistic and psychological studies which it generated.

After summarizing many of the studies, Christopherson concludes with a summary and a statement of hypotheses. (Note: Researchers often use *problem* statement and *hypothesis* interchangeably.)

This review of relevant linguistic, psycholinguistic, and psychology literature indicates that semantic roles can be used to describe the structure and content of language and that semantic roles are significant elements in reconstructive memory. These findings suggest that readers who are taught semantic roles might be expected to have a greater awareness of the structure and content of prose as they read and that they would be able to reconstruct more completely what they have read. The experiment reported here concerns the effects of readers' knowledge of semantic roles on their recall of connected prose.

Hypotheses

1. Readers who are taught semantic roles will have better immediate recall of prose than a control group of readers who are not taught semantic roles.

2. Readers who are taught semantic roles will have better delayed recall of prose than a control group of readers who are not taught semantic roles.

3. The influence of knowledge of semantic roles will occur at the time of reading rather than at the time of recall.

What were the characteristics of the subject population that was used?

In the Method section, Christopherson describes the materials and subjects:

Materials

The prose material for this experiment consisted of five passages which were patterned after short reports in the "Science and the Citizen" section of *Scientific American*. Each passage contained 331 to 336 words.

Subjects

Thirty-four unpaid volunteers were recruited for this experiment at Cornell University and were randomly assigned to either the experimental or the control group. All but five of the thirty-four volunteers (three experimental and two control) were able to return for a second meeting one week after the first meeting. The sex and age of participants who finished the experiment were similar for the two groups; the experimental group had ten women and four men, with an average age of 17.6 years, and the control group had nine women and six men, with an average of 17.9 years.

A difficult problem is the loss of subjects in experiments. If the losses are substantially greater in one group, the results may be impossible to interpret. That is, the subjects in the greater-loss group might have had some characteristics (such as motivation) that affected their performance in the experimental tasks.

What are the independent and dependent variables?
Was the independent variable actually manipulated?
What was the design of the experiment?

Christopherson describes the designs and procedures next:

Design and Procedures

Each participant met individually with the experimenter. In the first meeting, each subject read all five passages in one of five different orders. The position of each passage was balanced so that each passage appeared in each position. The first three passages were used for practice, and the last two passages were used for testing the hypotheses.

Each participant was read instructions by the experimenter. After reading and recalling the first passage, each participant in the experimental groups was told that semantic roles help readers analyze and organize the information in a passage and thereby improve recall. Participants in the experimental group were then taught the following seven semantic roles: Agent (who or what caused the event), Patient (who or what was directly affected by the event), Instrument (what was used to perform the event), Location (where the event took place), Benetive (who or what benefitted or suffered from the event), Factitive (what was the outcome of the event), and Essive (what descriptions and identifications were given). These semantic roles were illustrated with samples from the first passage. The experimental subjects then read and recalled the second passage, the third passage, and the fourth passage. After each recall, the roles were again briefly illustrated with examples from the passage just recalled.

Like the experimental participants, the control participants read and recalled the first passage without any special instructions. The control participants were then asked to skim over the first passage and were told that this "feedback" was intended to help improve their recall of subsequent passages by giving them an idea of the sorts of information they tend to remember and the sorts they tend to leave out. The control participants then read and recalled the second, third, and fourth passages. After each recall, they skimmed the passage for "feedback."

The fifth passage was read by both groups but was not recalled immediately. A stopwatch, which the subjects had not seen before, was pulled from under cover as soon as each subject finished reading the last passage. All of the participants were told that the purpose of the final passage had been to find out how their practice with the earlier passages had affected their reading rates. Then they were asked to return in one week for a "similar" session. Upon returning, each participant was asked to recall the fifth passage and then the first passage.

While it is not explicitly stated, the experiment uses a two-group design. The independent variable is the amount of instruction in semantic roles. Note that this is an experiment in that the teaching of semantic roles *is* manipulated.

Christopherson describes the dependent variable and the scoring of the recall data next:

All recall protocols were blindly and leniently scored for idea units. The lenient scoring meant that a subject was given credit for recalling an idea unit even if only part of it, such as a noun or verb, was recalled. Each score in this experiment was a ratio of the number of idea units recalled to the total number of idea units. As a reliability check, one-fourth of the protocols were rescored after six months, yielding a reliability coefficient of $r = .97$.

The reliability check indicates that the scoring procedure was not capricious. (Reliability is discussed in chapter 3.)

How were the data analyzed?
Were the results statistically significant?

The Results section describes the data analysis and test of the hypothesis:

Results

Hypotheses one and two, regarding the effects of knowledge of semantic roles on immediate and delayed recall, were tested by comparing the scores of the treatment and control groups on the immediate recall of the fourth passage and on the delayed recall of the fifth passage. An analysis of the immediate recall of the fourth passage gave nonsignificant support for the hypothesis that the experimental group would score higher than the control group on immediate recall $t(32) = .874$, $p < .20$. The mean proportions of idea units recalled immediately were .447 and .405 for the experimental and control groups, respectively. In the test of hypothesis two, the experimental group scored significantly higher than the control group on the delayed recall of the fifth passage, $t(27) = 2.01$, $p < .05$. The mean proportions of idea units recalled for the fifth passage after one week were .219 and .137 for the experimental and control groups, respectively.

A comparison of the experimental and control groups' delayed recall of the first passage provided a test of hypothesis three, that the influence of semantic roles would occur during the reading of a passage, rather than during recall. The first passage was read by both groups without any tutoring; the immediate, untutored recall of the first passage, therefore, should be similar for the two groups. The mean immediate recall scores were found to be nearly identical: .311 and .314 for the experimental and control groups, respectively. The delayed recall of the first passage occurred after tutoring. If the benefit from the knowledge of semantic roles occurs during reading, rather than retroactively during recall, then the delayed recall of the first passage would also be similar for the two groups. If the benefit occurs, instead, during recall, then the experimental group's delayed recall would be significantly better than the control group's. An analysis of the delayed recall of the first passage revealed no difference between the groups, $t(27) = .21, p < .83$, in support of hypothesis three. The mean proportions of idea units recalled after one week for the first passage were .285 and .274 for the experimental and control groups, respectively.

Note that while the probability level of the first is $p < 0.20$, Christopherson deems the differences nonsignificant. As noted earlier, conventional procedures dictate the use of $p < 0.05$ (or smaller) to establish significance level. One other point is illustrated in the passage: The means for the two groups should always be reported. This allows the reader to know what the performance levels were.

Are the results educationally or psychologically significant?
Are the results related back to theory or prior work?

In the Discussion section, Christopherson indicates what he feels the results mean:

A comparison between the two treatment groups on immediate recall slightly favored the experimental group, but the difference was not statistically significant. The difference of .042 between the means of the two groups on the fourth recall represented a ten percent advantage of the experimental group's recall over the control group's recall.

The experimental group remembered a significantly higher proportion of the material on delayed recall than did the control group. The difference between the two means represented a sixty percent advantage of the experimental group over the control group, whereas the initial, untutored recall showed that the two groups began at essentially identical levels of performance. A comparison of the two groups' attitudes toward their treatments showed that the difference in delayed recall could not be accounted for by a difference in expectations; it was the control group, rather than the experimental group that had slightly, but insignificantly, more positive attitudes.

A general explanation of the improvement in delayed recall of the fifth passage may be that teaching semantic roles to readers improves recall by improving comprehension; what linguists have found useful for describing language, readers may find useful for understanding language.

Are the implications limited to the conditions of the experiment?

Christopherson has related the experiment to prior theory and work. He indicates the psychological importance and then proceeds to ask questions that would, if verified, lead to educational applications:

> This study provides further evidence of the psychological importance of semantic roles for verbal learning and broadens the realm of earlier work with semantic roles by using connected prose rather than individual sentences. It also raises a number of unanswered questions for further study. Through what process or processes does the knowledge of semantic roles facilitate reading recall? Does knowledge of semantic roles facilitate processes which naive readers are also using, or are other processes activated? If overt, tutored use of semantic roles improves reading and recall, would differences in covert, unintentional use of semantic roles differentiate naive good and poor readers?

The questions left unanswered by this study illustrate the cumulative nature of experimental research. Future work on this topic by Christopherson or other researchers should use these questions—and the conclusions of this study and those that preceded it—as a guide. Before the results of this study can be translated into educational practice, much more work needs to be done.

In Conclusion

Simple experimental designs were once very common in educational research. Today, researchers tend not to use them, preferring to study more complex clusters of educational processes. We presented this example to clarify the basic concepts in experimental research. In more complex designs, the manipulations can be reduced to combinations of concepts demonstrated in the simple design presented here. This is true for the design of complex studies, as well as for the analyses.

IN SUMMARY

Experimental research shows causal links between variables and outcomes. It follows the rules of the scientific method in which hypotheses are generated, tested, revised, and retested. Simple experimental designs establish causal links between *one* variable and its outcome. Since most educational processes involve many variables, each contributing to the end result, the use of simple designs is infrequent.

REFERENCES

Bronfenbrenner, U. (1976). The experimental ecology for education. *Educational Researcher, 5*, 5–15.

Campbell, D., & Stanley, J. (1966). *Experimental and quasi-experimental designs for research*. Chicago: Rand-McNally.

Christopherson, S. (1978). Effects of knowledge of semantic roles on recall of written prose. *Journal of Reading Behavior, 10*, 249–256.

Chapter 7

The Logic
of Experimental Research:
Complex Designs

In the last chapter, we considered experiments in which only two conditions—control and experimental—were used. In this chapter, we will consider situations in which researchers make the experiment more like the real world.

As we noted in the last chapter, the ecological validity of a research study is a function of the number of variables the study accounts for. We know that single variables rarely operate in isolation. The use of complex designs allows researchers to manipulate several factors simultaneously. Conclusions about research results can then be made in terms of the effects of groups of variables and their *interactions*.

QUESTIONS FOR COMPLEX DESIGNS

The questions developed in chapter 6 on simple designs are equally appropriate here. Refer to them in the course of this chapter.

The major differences in reading and analyzing complex designs, as opposed to simple ones, will be in the answers to those questions. For example, complex designs usually have more complicated statistical analyses, more chances for experimental errors, and more involved conclusions. We will describe situations in which there is a single independent variable with several values and situations in which there are several different independent variables used in a design or plan for conducting the experiment.

Because the principles are so much like those for simple designs, we will present only partial reports in this chapter. If more information is desired, refer to the uncited portions of these reports.

One Independent Variable
with Several Values

Often we want to know more about the effects of single independent variables than we can find out from two-group experiments. We may want to know what happens when we use several other values of the independent variable. For example, we might want to find out what the optimum amount of instruction using a certain method might be. A reasonable design might be to use a control group that received no instruction in the method, a second group that received a moderate amount, and a final group that received intensive instruction.

On the basis of the data, a researcher would be able to conclude whether the results were due to comparing the teaching method against nothing, or whether the amount of instruction in the method was important. Many of the same problems that can occur with two-group designs remain, however. The experiment is not valid if there are differences among the groups *before* the study begins. The same *control* problems remain. They are, however, intensified, since there are more groups. The solutions are similar to the solutions for two groups.

Statistical Analysis

The most commonly used statistical procedure for analyzing results in the situations described above is called a *one-way analysis of variance*. It is called *one-way* because there is only *one* dependent variable or *factor*. It is an *analysis of variance* because the statistic is based on comparisons of the variances of the groups. We use the variances to make inferences about whether the differences among the means could have been due to chance. That is, we use the differences in the spread of scores (variance) to determine how likely it is that the means are truly different.

There are two steps in the statistical analysis. In the first step, a statistic called an F ratio is calculated. This is a numerical quantity that relates the amount of variance in the data to specific sources of variance, like that due to a treatment. When the variances are unequal, the data are believed to come from different populations. In the second step, if the null hypothesis is rejected, we examine specific differences among pairs or groups of the means. As with t-tests, a null hypothesis is generated. The null hypothesis is that all the means are equal:

$$H_0: \mu_1 = \mu_2 = \ldots = \mu_g \, ,$$

where g is the number of groups and μ is the population mean.

That is, the hypothesis to be tested states that there is no difference among the groups. The alternative hypothesis is that there *is* at least one difference.

The statistic is reported, for example, as:

$$F(2,29) = 7.89, p < .05 .$$

The numbers inside the parentheses are the degrees of freedom (df), similar in function to those for *t*-tests. There are two numbers here: The first indicates the df for the number of groups (in this case, 3 groups yield 2 df), and the second represents the df for the number of subjects used. In general, the larger the degrees of freedom, the smaller the differences between the means can be and still be statistically significant. This ability to detect differences in the samples of data is called the *power* of a statistical test. The larger the degrees of freedom, the greater the power. The probability value indicates that the differences that produced this statistic would occur by chance fewer than 5 times out of 100.

When *F* ratios are not significant, the statistic is often reported as $F(3,81) < 1.00$. In order for *any F* ratio to be significant, it has to be greater than 1.0.

Subsequent Tests

If the *F* ratio is not significant, there is little more to be done. The conclusion is that any differences observed in the experimental situation were most likely due to chance. If, however, the hypothesis is rejected, then we are left with the conclusion that at least one of the group means was different from the others. The experimenter finds out which mean was different by using subsequent tests.

A variety of subsequent tests are commonly used. The conceptually simplest procedure is a version of the *t*-test discussed in the previous chapter. A researcher may perform *t*-tests on any *pair* of means. Doing so will pinpoint the differences among the set of means. For instance, in the example mentioned above, the difference between the control group and the moderate instruction group *might not* be significant, while the difference between the control and the intensive instruction groups might have been.

Other subsequent tests in common use are the Newman-Keuls, the Tukey procedure, the Duncan Test, and the Scheffé procedure. (Discussions of these tests can be found in Shavelson 1981.) Some of these allow the researcher to make comparisons among sets (for example, testing the control group against *all* the other groups), rather than only between pairs. All of these tests introduce some safeguards against making statistical errors. The more statistical tests one performs, the more likely a statistic will be significant by accident. (Remember, these are probabilities, not certainties.) By changing the ways in which the statistical values are calculated or compared, each test guards against errors.

As you read experimental research of this sort, look carefully in the Results section for the group means, the variances or standard deviations associated with the means, the statistical values, and the subsequent tests used. Knowing there was a difference among the groups does not tell you how large it was. By inspecting the means (when the differences are statistically significant), you can obtain this information.

Another index of educational significance is called *effect size*. This is an index of the amount of variance that can be accounted for in a set of data by a specific variable. We will discuss these in more detail later in this chapter. (Effect sizes are also discussed more in chapter 8 and chapter 9.)

An Example

Carnine, Kameenui, and Woolfson (1982) were interested in studying the effects of text dimensions and training strategies on readers' abilities to make inferences.

> *What is the problem being studied?*
> *What is the hypothesis?*

To make the problem manageable, they had to state the problem in specific terms:

> In attempting to carefully look at the effects of specific textual dimensions and precise interventions on a particular type of inference behavior, much was sacrificed in terms of generalizability. First, one particular narrow definition of inference was selected—deductions based on an artificial rule. Second, the systematic manipulation of the various textual dimensions resulted in highly contrived passages. Third, the instructional materials (structurally similar, single passages) and instructional presentations (individual) did not represent typical classroom practice. Limitations of this type sometimes characterize initial studies in relatively new areas because of efforts to maximize internal validity and test specific hypotheses. Subsequent studies could attend to external validity, in this case, incorporating a greater variety of inferences derived from naturalistic prose and presented in typical classroom settings.

> *What are the independent and dependent variables?*
> *What were the characteristics of the subject population?*

The same authors describe their subject population, setting, and materials:

Method

Subjects and Setting

Middle-class fifth-graders from two classrooms were selected to participate in the study based on (1) their ability to accurately and fluently read three screening stories, and (2) on their failure to answer the inference question specific to each of the three screening stories. Subjects who read the stories accurately and fluently but missed the inference question for two or three stories were selected as subjects. Students who paused between words when reading, or who answered the question at the end of the story accurately for two or more of the three screening items, were excluded from the subject pool. The first 36 eligible fifth-graders were randomly assigned to one of three groups.

Materials

Nine stories of approximately 250 words in length were used in the study. Three were used for screening. These three stories plus three more were used for training, resulting in six training stories. The three final stories were used for the transfer test. In all nine stories the components appeared in the same order: problem statement, irrelevant information, rule, distractors, less obvious critical information, and finally the questions that called for text-based inference.

Note that the random assignment of subjects to treatment (experimental) groups is one of the marks of experimental research. Without such random assignment, some systematic bias might be introduced into the data collection.

Was the independent variable actually manipulated?
What was the design of the experiment?

While Carnine, Kameenui, and Woolfson did not include a section specifically labelled "Design," they do describe the three groups, two of which received specific instruction. The third group was a control group and received no treatment.

Procedure

Systematic Instruction Group. Training was conducted in three sessions on three consecutive days. Two of the six training stories were read each session. The transfer test was administered following the final day of training.

Several detailed sequential steps, reflecting a prompted questioning strategy, were followed with the first story. The steps involved identifying the various components in the story, beginning with the problem statement and finishing with the text-based inference. The trainer asked sequential questions of the subject to elicit identification of the components of the story. The experimenter used a whole word corrections procedure to correct any words that were misread (e.g., "Stop, what word? That word is ___."). Scripted corrections were followed whenever a student missed an experimenter question.

Following the three training sessions, the subject received a transfer test. The subject read three stories during the transfer session. The stories were composed of the same components and sequenced in the same order as the training items. The subject read a story and responded to the question posed at the end of each story. The subject received no assistance on the transfer stories.

Corrective Feedback Group. The subject was instructed to read the story and to answer the question at the end of the story. The experimenter corrected any misread words by providing a whole word correction. If the subject responded correctly to the question at the end of the story, the experimenter asked why s/he made that choice. If the subject was able to cite verbally or point to the problem statement, rule, and/or indirect information, s/he was praised. If the subject responded incorrectly, the experimenter provided corrective feedback by supplying the correct answer. For example: "No. He chose the small carrots because they were fresher." This procedure was repeated for all six training stories.

Each subject received training in three training sessions over three consecutive days. Two stories were read each session. The transfer test was administered following the final day of training.

No Intervention Control Group. The Control Group did not receive any training. Subjects assigned to this group participated only in the screening and transfer test sessions.

The design can be inferred from the Procedure section. There were three groups of twelve subjects each.

> *How were the data analyzed?*
> *Were the results statistically significant?*

The Results section is brief, but it contains all the relevant information:

Results

The means (with a maximum of three correct responses) were 1.9 (SD = .95) for the Systematic Instruction Group, .7 (SD = .78) for the Corrective Feedback Group and .6 (SD = 1.0) for the Control Group. According to a one-way ANOVA, there was a significant difference among the means, $F(2,33) = 8.5$, $p < .005$. (Assumptions of the homogeneity of variances were not violated, Bartlett-Box $F = .35$, $p < .7$). The Scheffé post-hoc test for multiple comparisons indicated that the mean of the Systematic Instruction group ($p < .05$) was significantly higher than the means for the other groups.

The means were given in terms of number of correct questions answered for the *three* stories combined. Looking at the means suggests that the *Systematic Instruction group* did better than the others; the ANOVA confirms that at least one of the means for the three groups was different from the others. The Bartlett-Box test is used to determine whether the variances of the groups are similar or not. If they are not (that is, the F-ratio would be significant), the statistical procedure used is inappropriate. It is nonsignificant here, indicating that all the scores probably came from similar populations. It was appropriate to use the ANOVA procedure. Finally, the Scheffé test confirms the impression that the difference between the mean for *Systematic Instruction* and that for the other groups was statistically significant.

This type of design could be extended to include as many values of the variable of interest as necessary. For example, Bond and Hayes (in press) used five different conditions of text to study the ability of students to create paragraphs.

More Than One
Independent Variable

The real world of education typically does not work in a way that allows researchers to study a single variable without considering others. Complex experimental designs can allow the simultaneous manipulation of two or more variables. A researcher can then determine what the joint effects of the variables will be. In other words, a researcher can begin to approximate real-world situations by studying a number of variables at one time.

We can see the first major difference between simple and more complex experiments when *factorial* designs are used. A factorial design is one in which every level of every variable is combined with every level of all other variables. To illustrate this, we can use the design from a study by Collins and Williamson (1981) in which they examined the effects of spoken language on semantic abbreviation (inadequate representation of situational and cultural contexts in writing).

To investigate this problem, Collins and Williamson used two independent variables, writing ability and grade level (see Figure 7–1). This design shows that each level of each variable appears with all the levels of the other. That is, strong writers were found at each of the three grades; weak writers were also found at each of the three grades.

A complete factorial design can have many factors or variables, and each variable can have different numbers of levels or values from the others. One place to find this information is in the description of design in the Method section of a report. Vosniadou and Ortony (1983) describe their design:

> The design was (2 × 2) × (2) factorial design with Grade (first vs third grade) and Group (Analogy vs No Analogy) as between-subject variables, and Passage (Blood Circulation vs Infection) as a within-subject variable.

What we know immediately is that there are three variables, each with two levels. *Between-subjects* variables are those in which different subjects are used at each level of the variable. In this example, Grade was one

Figure 7–1
Levels of independent variables: Writing ability and grade level

Grade Level

	4	8	12
Strong			
Weak			

Writing Ability Level

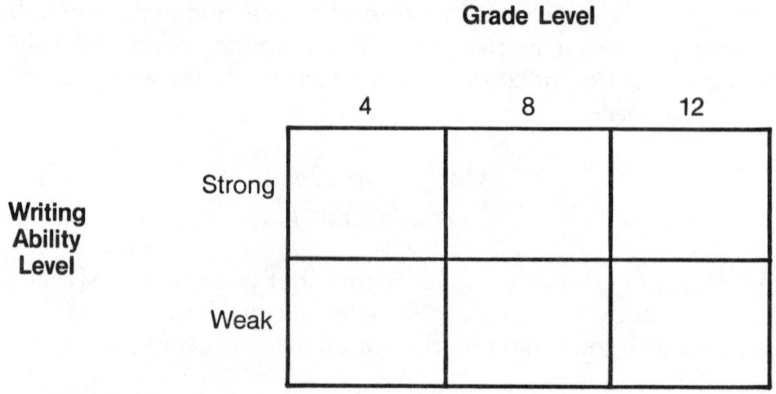

between-subjects variable, because the first-grade students *had* to be different from the third-grade students.

Within-subject variables are those in which the same subjects are used at each level. Passage was between subjects because each subject received *both* passages. Often within-subject variables are referred to as *repeated-measure* variables.

Another example of a complex design is seen in Reynolds and Schwartz (1983):

> *What are the independent and dependent variables?*
> *Was the independent variable actually manipulated?*
> *What was the design of the experiment?*

> The design was a 2 (recall interval: immediate vs. 7-day delay) × 2 (cue type: precue vs. postcue) × 2 (target type: metaphor vs. literal equivalent) × 8 (passage) factorial design, with recall interval, cue type, and target type as between-subject factors, and passage as a within-subject factor. The dependent measure was the amount of recall on the cued recall test.

There are not really any theoretical limits on the number of factors or levels of factors in a design. However, as a practical matter, consider that a research study needs to have several different subjects receive each combination of treatments. For example, a 2 × 2 design has 4 cells; each replication requires 4 subjects. If we have a 2 × 2 × 2 design, there are 8 cells, and replications require 8 subjects. Thus, very complex designs may require many subjects and a great deal of time to complete, particularly when the variables are between subjects. The more between-subjects variables there are in a design, the more subjects are required for the completion of the study.

Between- versus
Within-Subject Variables

Before we turn to the analysis of these complex designs, we must consider the relative merits of choosing between- or within-subject variables. Each choice has advantages, as well as disadvantages. In some instances, the choices are determined by the nature of the variables. For example, reading ability has to be a between-subjects variable, since each subject can only be placed in one value (for instance, good or poor) of the variable.

Between-subjects variables require a different set of subjects at every value. Within-subject variables are thus more economical in this regard. To study improvement over time, measures are repeated on the same subjects; this is not possible in between-subjects designs. Other sorts of concerns can also dictate the choice of within- or between-subject designs.

If different treatments (along the same variable dimension) are similar, using the same subjects in all treatments might introduce carryover or contrast effects; subjects might perform differently as a result of having had one or another of the treatments. Any differences between the groups of subjects might be due to the different treatments or because of the *order* of those treatments. In reading research that uses experimental designs, be certain about which variables are between and which are within subjects. The author should offer a rationale for the choices made in any research design.

Results Obtained from Using the Main Effects of Complex Designs

As with one-factor designs, the most common method of analysis is the ANOVA. There are additional complications, however, when the design includes more than one variable. For each variable, there is a hypothesis—namely, that there is no difference between the levels along that variable. This is usually referred to as a test of a *main effect*. If a main effect is found to be significant, then subsequent test procedures should be used to determine which values are different from each other.

Some Examples

It is important to understand that the hypotheses for the tests of main effects may not be precisely stated. They are assumed to be implicit in each analysis. That is, for each main effect, a significant F ratio indicates that at least one value along that variable dimension is different from the others. Gould (1978) reports that:

> Highly experienced dictators were 50–66% faster at dictating than at writing. Dictating and speaking were significantly faster than writing and invisible writing, $F(3,21) = 11.83$, $p < .001$ (Duncan's Multiple range test, $p < .01$).

This means that of the four conditions used, dictating and speaking were both faster than conditions in which participants had to compose letters by writing or invisible writing (where they could not see what they were writing). The main effect indicates that *at least* one condition was different from the others. The report of the Duncan's multiple-range statistic indicates (in this instance) that the two pairs of conditions were significantly different from each other.

Another illustration comes from Reynolds and Schwartz (1983). They report:

For the verbatim measure, significant main effects were found for target-type, $F(1,15) = 7.23$, $p < .05$, and passage, $F(7,105) = 4.06$, $p < .01$. The target-type result was due to greater recall of the metaphors than the literally equivalent statements. No other results reached significance, all $ps > .20$.

It is common to report F ratios only for the statistically significant effects. The authors acknowledge that they have done a complete analysis by summarizing all the nonsignificant effects in one sentence.

Interactions

In addition to the tests of main effects, complex designs allow the tests for *interactions*. An interaction between two variables occurs when the effects of one variable change at the different levels of the other variable. An example from Goetz, Schallert, Reynolds, and Radin (1983) shows one type of interaction.

In this study, the effects of different cognitive perspectives on comprehension were analyzed. Participants in the study were asked to assume the perspective of a burglar or a homebuyer before reading a passage describing a house. The passage contained sentences that would be of interest to a burglar (presence of jewelry) or to a homebuyer (presence of a new furnace). In one portion of the study, the subjects were asked to rate the importance of the sentences in the passages. The results are presented in Figure 7–2.

Figure 7–2
Importance ratings of sentences in Goetz, Schallert, Reynolds, and Radin (1983)

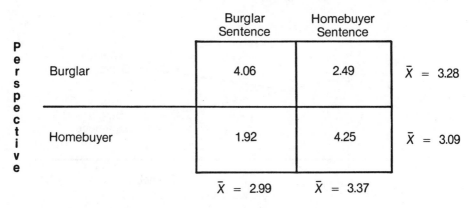

Source: Adapted from Goetz, Schallert, Reynolds, and Radin 1983, 504 (Table 1).

These same sentence-rating data are shown in Figure 7–3. In the example here, the interaction *is* statistically significant. Consequently, the effect of taking a burglar perspective is different for the sentence types from taking a homebuyer perspective. This can be seen in Figure 7–3, since the lines cross. If there were no interaction, the effects of taking a particular perspective would be the same for rating either homebuyer or burglar sentences. Goetz et al. report:

> The Perspective × Sentence Type intersection repli-
> cated Pichert and Anderson's (1977) major findings,
> $F(2,89) = 16.1$, $p < .001$, $MS_e = .013$.

This means that there is less than 1 chance out of 1,000 that the findings shown in Figure 7–3 occurred by chance. The term MS_e is an estimate of the overall variance that cannot be associated with any other variable, main effect, or interaction. To illustrate a nonsignificant interaction, Figure 7–4 shows a graph of a hypothetical set of data. Note that the lines in this figure are parallel.

Interactions can occur between two variables or more, up to the number of variables in a given design. Thus, in the Goetz et al. example, there is a perspective × sentence type two-way interaction. If there were three variables, there could be three-way interaction. We cannot determine visually whether the lines are precisely parallel, particularly when there are more than two variables. Therefore, interactions must be subjected to statistical tests as well. As with main effects, the hypotheses underlying the statistical tests of interactions are implicit rather than overtly stated.

Figure 7–3
Mean sentence ratings as a function of perspective

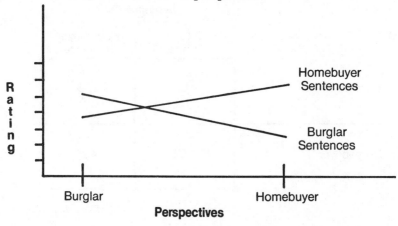

Source: Adapted from Goetz, Schallert, Reynolds, and Radin 1983, 504 (Table 1).

Figure 7–4
Hypothetical set of data in which there is no interaction

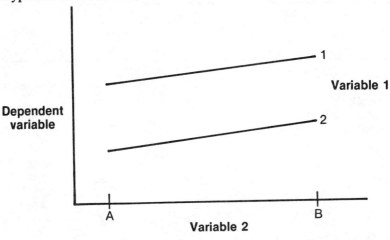

Summary Tables

In some instances, results of complex analyses of variance are reported in summary tables. An example of this can be seen in Table 7–1, from Freedman and Calfee (1983).

Freedman and Calfee were interested in the effects of rewriting on the ratings of essays. The categories were those listed in Table 7–1 under Writing Factors. When examining a summary table, be careful to determine whether *all* sources are accounted for. In this example, Freedman and Calfee state (referring to the table):

> First, there are the four rewriting factors that were the focus of the study. Next on the list are several interactions that were selected as especially interesting—these measure the extent to which the effect of one of the rewriting factors varied from level to level of another rewriting factor. Below the interactions are several sources associated with the raters. First, there is the main effect of the raters themselves—this source measures variability that is due to overall differences in level of judgment (Did some raters give consistently higher or lower ratings than others?). Second, there are the interactions between raters and rewriting factors. These sources measure individual differences in the effect of each rewriting factor—if all twelve raters reacted in a similar fashion to the contrast between the strong and weak versions along a particular di-

Table 7–1
Analysis of variance for holistic scores: Rewriting effects

Source	Degrees of Freedom (df)	Mean Square	F Ratio
Writing Factors			
Development (D)	1	9.86	31.70[b]
Organization (O)	1	5.20	16.70[b]
Sentence Structure (SS)	1	1.50	4.82
Mechanics (M)	1	5.04	16.21[b]
Writing Interaction			
D x SS	1	1.96	6.30
D x M	1	.99	3.18
O x SS	1	3.77	12.11[a]
O x M	1	6.16	19.78[b]
SS x M	1	.00	0
Reader and Reader Interactions			
Reader (R)	11	.45	
R x D	11	.26	
R x O	11	.18	
R x SS	11	.59	
R x M	11	.52	
Residual	31	.31	

[a] $p < .01$ 1,31 df $F = 7.56$
[b] $p < .001$ 1,31 df $F = 13.29$
Note: F is based on residual error variance.
Source: Freedman and Calfee 1983, 88. Used with permission.

mension, the rater interaction with this factor would
be small, and contrariwise.

Freedman and Calfee present only a portion of the possible sources
of variance. The F ratios for the Reader and Reader Interactions are not
presented in the table, since they are nonsignificant *and* difficult to interpret. That is, one would expect differences to occur between individuals,
even though the present differences are small.

When it comes to the interpretation of the ANOVA, Freedman and
Calfee limit themselves to the sources of variation listed in the table. They
write:

The results in [Table 7–1] support several important
conclusions. First, three of the four rewriting factors

strongly influenced the raters' judgments; development had the greatest effect, followed by organization and mechanics. Sentence structure was not a statistically significant factor, although the results were in the predicted direction. Second, although most of the systematic variability was attributable to the main effects, two interactions noticeably influenced the judgments. Both of the interactions involved the organization factor. If an essay was well organized, the ratings were clearly higher if the sentence structure and mechanics were also in good shape. However, if an essay had a weak organization, neither the sentence structure nor mechanics factors had much effect on the ratings. Finally, all of the rater sources were of roughly the same order of magnitude; individual differences were small among this sample of raters, who had been selected to be fairly homogeneous.

We have seen how to read and interpret both simple and complex ANOVAs. Now we will examine some of the other designs used in conducting experimental research.

Other Designs

Many varieties of complex experimental design are used to solve specific control or other problems. These are not the most common designs, and there are so many alternatives that we do not have space to deal with all of them in a complete manner. A list of references is included if you want to learn more about some of these designs.

When sequences of problems are used as an experimental treatment, the order should be changed for different subjects. If there are more than two or three items in a sequence, the number of different orders becomes extremely large. (For example, for 2 items, there are 2 sequences; for 3 items, 6 sequences; for 4, 24 sequences.) One solution is to use a *Latin Square* design. A Latin Square represents a balanced set of sequences in which every problem appears in every position in a sequence equally often. An example of a Latin Square for an experiment in which subjects read passages is given in Figure 7–5. Additional examples can be found in designs used by Gipe (1978–79), who studied vocabulary acquisition, and Gould (1978), who studied composition of letters.

Partial factorial designs are used when researchers have no interest in certain combinations of treatments. While this is not at all a common design, discussions of these designs include Calfee (1982) and Calfee and Piontkowski (1984).

Figure 7-5
A Latin Square design for an experiment in which each subject reads four passages

Passages

	A	C	B	D
	D	B	A	C
Sequences	C	A	D	B
	B	D	C	A

Analysis of covariance can be used to substitute for some situations in which measures might be confounded. For example, the effects of reading instruction might be greater on children who had larger vocabularies at the start of a study. Rowe and Cunningham (1983) studied the effects of instructional strategies on kindergartners' concept of words. They used vocabulary knowledge as a covariate for the final measures. That is, they statistically adjusted performance to account for different beginning levels of word knowledge, since they were probably *not* equal to begin with.

Cautions about Statistical Analyses

While most experimental work is analyzed by either ANOVAs, *t*-tests, or some form of multiple regression, this is not always the case. If the data do not meet certain assumptions (for instance, that variances are approximately normal), it may be inappropriate to use an ANOVA. In these cases, researchers may resort to other statistics for which the assumptions are not as strict. These tests are called *nonparametric* because they do not require the data to conform to certain assumptions. Common among these are the Mann-Whitney U, the Wilcoxon test, and the Signs test. It is difficult to judge the quality of a piece of experimental research by the statistical procedures used, even when they are unusual. However, nonparametric tests are often not as powerful as other tests.

Statistical versus
Educational Significance

We have stressed the interpretation of statistical significance. A number of researchers believe that results can only have educational significance if they are replicable. At the very least, they insist that measures of effect size (see chapter 8 and chapter 9) should be calculated for all statistically significant findings.

For example, Wixson (1983) reports a significant difference among passages used in a study of postreading questions. However, she indicates:

> Effect sizes were calculated using a conditional eta-squared (η^2), as defined by $SS_{effect} / (SS_{effect} + SS_{error})$. Although the passage effect was reliable, it accounts for 6% of the variance in the children's answers, which makes it a very weak effect.

In many journals, authors are routinely required to report some measure of effect size. In general, statistical significance is meaningful in terms of educational significance when the effect sizes are large.

IN SUMMARY

When researchers know a great deal about an area, experimental research is particularly useful in determining specific relationships between sets of variables. There is always the danger that generalizations from experiments may not be possible. Too often unforeseen variables affect the conduct of experiments. When that is the case, experimental methods are usually self-correcting, as explained in the previous chapter. The choices of designs, variables, and even materials all make it difficult to discover the realities of improving educational practice. Experimental research is one powerful tool that can aid researchers in this endeavor.

REFERENCES

Bond, S., & Hayes, J. (In press). Cues people use to paragraph text. *Research in the Teaching of English.*

Calfee, R. (1982). Applications of experimental design principles to research on reading instruction. In J. Niles & L. Harris (Eds.), *New inquiries in reading research and instruction* (Thirty-first yearbook of the National Reading Conference). Rochester, NY: The National Reading Conference.

Calfee, R., & Piontkowski, D. (1984). Design and analysis of experiments. In P. D. Pearson (Ed.), *Handbook of reading research.* New York: Longman.

Carnine, D., Kameenui, E., & Woolfson, W. (1982). Training of textual dimensions related to text-based inferences. *Journal of Reading Behavior, 14,* 335–340.

Collins, J., & Williamson, M. (1981). Spoken language and semantic abbreviation in writing. *Research in the Teaching of English, 15,* 23–35.

Freedman, S., & Calfee, R. (1983). Holistic assessment of writing: Experimental design and cognitive theory. In P. Mosenthal, L. Tamor, & S. Walmsley (Eds.), *Research on writing: Principles and methods.* New York: Longman.

Gipe, J. (1978–79). Investigating techniques for teaching word meaning. *Reading Research Quarterly, 14,* 624–644.

Goetz, E., Schallert, D., Reynolds, R., & Radin, D. (1983). Reading in perspective: What real cops and pretend burglars look for in a story. *Journal of Educational Psychology, 75,* 500–510.

Gould, J. (1978). How experts dictate. *Journal of Experimental Psychology: Human Perception and Performance, 4,* 648–661.

Leslie, L., & Jett-Simpson, M. (1983). The effects of recall instructions and story deletions on children's story comprehension. In J. Niles and L. Harris (Eds.), *Searches for meaning in reading, language processing, and instruction* (Thirty-second yearbook of the National Reading Conference). Rochester, NY: The National Reading Conference.

Reynolds, R., & Schwartz, R. (1983). Relation of metaphoric processing to comprehension and memory. *Journal of Educational Psychology, 75,* 450–459.

Rowe, D., & Cunningham, P. (1983). The effect of two instructional strategies on kindergartners' concept of word. In J. Niles (Ed.), *Searches for meaning in reading, language processing, and instruction* (Thirty-second yearbook of the National Reading Conference). Rochester, NY: The National Reading Conference.

Shavelson, R. (1981). *Statistical reasoning for the behavioral sciences.* Boston: Allyn and Bacon.

Vosniadou, S., & Ortony, A. (1983). The influence of analogy in children's acquisition of new information from text: An exploratory study. In J. Niles (Ed.), *Searches for meaning in reading, language processing, and instruction* (Thirty-second yearbook of the National Reading Conference). Rochester, NY: The National Reading Conference.

Wixson, K. (1983). Postreading question-answer interactions and children's learning from text. *Journal of Educational Psychology, 75,* 413–423.

ADDITIONAL EXAMPLES
OF EXPERIMENTAL STUDIES

Derry, S. (1984). Effects of an organizer on memory for prose. *Journal of educational psychology, 76,* 98–107.

Freebody, P., & Anderson, R. (1983). Effects of vocabulary difficulty, text cohesion, and schema availability on reading comprehension. *Reading Research Quarterly, 18,* 277–294.

Gould, J. (1978). An experimental study of writing, dictating, and speaking. In J. Requin (Ed.), *Attention and performance VII.* Hillsdale, NJ: Erlbaum.

Rayner, K., Carlson, M., & Frazier, L. (1983). The interaction of syntax and semantics during sentence processing: Eye movements in the analysis of semantically biased sentences. *Journal of Verbal Learning and Verbal Behavior, 22,* 358–374.

Roen, D., & Piché. (1984). The effects of selected text-forming structures on college freshmen's comprehension of expository prose. *Research in the Teaching of English, 18,* 8–25.

Taylor, B., & Beach, R. (1984). The effects of test structure instruction on middle-grade students' comprehension and production of text. *Reading Research Quarterly, 19,* 134–146.

ADDITIONAL READINGS
FOR EXPERIMENTAL METHODOLOGIES

Calfee, R. (1982). Applications of experimental design principles to research on reading instruction. In J. Niles & L. Harris (Eds.), *New inquiries in reading research and instruction* (Thirty-first yearbook of the National Reading Conference). Rochester, NY: The National Reading Conference.

Calfee, R. (1983). The design of reading research. *Journal of Reading Behavior, 15,* 59–80.

Calfee, R., & Piontkowski, D. (1984). Design and analysis of experiments. In P. D. Pearson, R. Barr, M. Kamil, & P. Mosenthal (Eds.), *Handbook of reading research* (pp. 63–90). New York: Longman.

Cook, T., & Campbell, D. (1979). *Quasi-experimentation: Design and analysis for field settings.* Chicago: Rand-McNally.

Dayton, C. (1970). *The design of educational experiments.* New York: McGraw-Hill.

Freedman, S., & Calfee, R. (1983). Holistic assessment of writing: Experimental design and cognitive theory. In P. Mosenthal, L. Tamor, S. Walmsley (Eds.), *Research on writing; Principles and methods.* New York: Longman.

Hardyck, C., & Petrinovich, L. (1975). *Understanding research in the social sciences.* Philadelphia: Saunders.

Kerlinger, F. (1973). *Foundations of behavioral research* (2nd edition). New York: Holt.

Kirk, R. (1968). *Experimental design: Procedures for the behavioral sciences.* Belmont, CA: Brooks/Cole.

Leonard, W., & Lowery, L. (1979). Was there really an experiment? *Educational Researcher, 6,* 4–7.

Lykken, D. (1968). Statistical significance in psychological research. *Psychological Bulletin, 70,* 151–159.

Myers, J. (1972). *Fundamentals of experimental design.* Boston: Allyn and Bacon.

Chapter 8

Multivariate Research

Multivariate analysis is being used with increasing frequency in reading and writing research. The term *multivariate analysis* refers to a collection of statistical techniques used to examine the relationships between three or more variables. These techniques are being used in place of the more traditional ANOVA techniques (discussed in chapter 7) because multivariate analysis offers the researcher a greater amount of flexibility in the design of studies and requires fewer arbitrary decisions (How do I differentiate good and poor readers? and the like). In addition, multivariate analysis has become easier to do because of the availability of computer programs capable of carrying out complex multivariate calculations inexpensively and efficiently. This type of analysis is relatively easy to perform and can be used to analyze many types of data to answer a variety of research questions. Multivariate analysis allows the researcher to examine a wide spectrum of categorical (sex, race, group, and so on) and continuous (IQ, reading scores, and so forth) variables. These statistical techniques can be employed to analyze data from descriptive or experimental studies in equally appropriate ways.

The purpose of this chapter is to familiarize the reader with some of the concepts, terminology, and statistics common to studies that use multivariate analysis. It is impossible for us to deal completely with all aspects of multivariate research, but we will examine the two types of research questions that can be answered through multivariate techniques. We will also provide a detailed examination of the most widely used multivariate technique (multiple regression) and less detailed treatments of some of the other multivariate techniques (factor analysis, MANOVA, and discriminant analysis). Finally, we will suggest specific guidelines to help the reader identify multivariate studies and enable him/her to examine such studies critically.

Although multivariate analysis is a type of data analysis and not a specific approach to research (that is, ethnographic, experimental, descriptive), it is reasonable to devote a chapter to the examination of research that uses multivariate analysis. This approach is taken for a number of reasons.

First, multivariate methodology is becoming increasingly prevalent in literacy and language research. Readers can expect to encounter many studies that use multivariate statistics. Second, the methodology of this type of analysis influences the nature of the questions that researchers ask and the types of data that they analyze. Traditional experiments—those that use analysis of variance (see chapters 6 and 7)—tend to be limited to the examination of highly constrained numbers of variables and conditions. Although experimental studies can be very useful in laboratory settings, they require the researcher to ignore many nonmanipulable variables (for instance, IQ, language skills, SES, sex, race, ethnic background, home environment, and so on) that might be operating in nonlaboratory settings, such as classrooms. Multivariate analysis allows the researcher to consider more complex explanations. Third, multivariate studies use terminology that is unique. To understand adequately such studies, it is necessary to understand the technical meanings of these terms and the conceptual meanings of the statistics. Finally, many multivariate analyses are subject to certain types of methodological or interpretive flaws that the reader must be aware of in order to interpret correctly the validity, reliability, and applicability of the reported findings.

MULTIVARIATE RESEARCH QUESTIONS

A number of analytical techniques fall under the rubric of multivariate analysis: multiple regression, discriminant analysis, canonical correlation, multivariate analysis of variance, factor analysis, and path analysis. Despite the variety of techniques available for performing multivariate research, there are only two types of problems that can be solved or questions that can be answered through the application of these statistical tools.

Measuring Relationships

First, multivariate techniques can be used to answer the question: What are the nature and magnitude of the relationships of dependent variables with two more more independent variables? Like ANOVA (chapter 7), multivariate techniques analyze the variance spread in scores and allow the researcher to relate this variance to the variation in other measures. Multivariate techniques are useful for solving this type of problem because they allow the researcher to divide, identify, and measure the sources and amounts of variation in the dependent measure.

When multivariate techniques are used to measure relationships, the researcher can, for example, find out about the conditions that result in certain outcomes. Walberg and Shanahan (1983), for instance, were able to use multivariate techniques to examine the relationship of high school reading achievement with a collection of home variables (such as parents' education, SES, parent interest, and amount of television viewing) and school variables (quality of instruction, quantity of academic instruction, school discipline, and so forth). This study found that variables such as parent interest in student learning, amount of academic instruction received, amount of homework, and amount of television viewing (a negative relationship) were important influences on student achievement. Similarly, a number of studies have been made to determine the features of student writing that influence teachers' evaluation of writing quality (Grobe 1981; Stewart and Leaman 1983). These studies found vocabulary diversity and word choice to be the major determinants of ratings, but length and spelling also had an influence. Such analyses permit the specification of conditions that determine the outcomes being examined. This is especially useful in studies such as these, because it probably would be impossible to manipulate experimentally all of the independent variables considered.

Simplifying Variable Sets

The second question that multivariate analysis can be used to answer is: How can we reduce large sets of variables to more manageable and efficient sets? This can be accomplished in two ways.

First, it is possible to simply measure the comparative effectiveness (that is, magnitudes of relationship with a dependent measure) of each of a large set of variables. This approach is especially useful for situations in which the researcher wants to make an efficient prediction.

An example of reducing variable sets is research done to identify an efficient formula for predicting success or failure in first-grade reading achievement (Jansky and de Hirsch 1972). If such a formula could be derived successfully, it would be possible to identify those children with a high risk of failure and to provide compensatory instruction to prevent learning problems. In such a case, the researcher wants to derive a very accurate prediction but wants to accomplish this with the fewest measures possible. Multivariate analysis is useful for reducing the costs of such prediction, because its techniques can be used to select the most powerful predictors from a large set of alternatives. Jansky and de Hirsch (1972) found that five measures from their original set of eighteen tests could be used to predict reading achievement as accurately as the entire set. The savings in using only five measures instead of eighteen would be substantial.

A second way that multivariate analysis can be used to make large sets of data more manageable is through *factor analysis,* a technique used to identify the factors or principle components that underlie a test or a set of tests. The researcher uses factor analysis in order to examine how the original tests combine to measure discrete abilities. That is, the interrelationships of the original variables are examined to find out how many independent dimensions or abilities are actually being assessed by the test(s). For example, using factor analysis, Davis (1983) examined a collection of 240 reading comprehension questions to determine the nature of the component abilities or skills of comprehension. On the basis of this analysis, Davis concluded that these 240 questions actually assessed only eight different comprehension abilities. (Other factor-analytic studies have challenged this finding. For a review of these studies, see Johnson, Toms-Bronowski, and Buss 1983). Factor analyses have been used to aid in test design and theory development in a number of areas, including the measurement of prereading knowledge or prior knowledge and its relationship to reading comprehension (Langer and Nicolich 1981); literary response (Zaharias and Mertz 1983); and writing instruction effectiveness (Witte, Daly, Faigley, and Koch 1983).

MULTIPLE REGRESSION

Accounting for Variance

Dividing, identifying, and measuring the sources and amounts of variance in dependent measures (accounting for variance) is probably the most common use of multivariate analysis in reading and writing research. *Multiple regression* is the multivariate technique used most frequently for this purpose. Regression allows the researcher to do many things, including the comparison of treatment and control groups. Regression is virtually identical to ANOVA (chapter 7) when used in this way. However, regression indicates not only whether group means differ significantly, but also provides an estimate of how much influence treatments or conditions have on specified outcomes. Regression explains or predicts the amount of variance in a dependent variable on the basis of its correlation with two or more independent variables. (For more on correlation, see chapter 3.) A regression simply measures the correlation that exists between a dependent measure and some set of independent variables. Although regression and correlation are conceptually identical, the use of three or more variables complicates the analysis and interpretation.

An Example of Variance Accounting

For example, assume that a researcher wants to find out which conditions contribute to children's development of print awareness. It will be necessary to collect some information about the children's background characteristics and experiences. To simplify matters, assume that the researcher is able to obtain only two pieces of information about the children in addition to the print awareness test itself: number of years of their parents' formal education and number of books available in their homes.

Once these data have been collected, the researcher can find out what relationship, if any, these background variables have with print awareness performance. One approach might be to calculate simple correlations separately for each of the background variables with the print awareness test scores. Such calculations might reveal, for example, that each of these variables has a 0.50 correlation with print awareness for this sample of children. Although the relationship of these variables to print awareness can be measured separately, it is doubtful that they actually influence print awareness development separately. For this reason, the researcher can rely on multiple regression to provide a more complete description of the relationship. Regression techniques allow the researcher to measure the simultaneous or combined influence these variables exert on print awareness.

If the two background variables were totally independent of each other, the simple correlational approach would be adequate. Figure 8–1, Part A illustrates the amount of overlap the two background variables share with print awareness. Because the two background variables do not overlap with each other, the relationship of these variables with print awareness can be measured unambiguously by adding their separate contributions or overlaps with print awareness. These background variables could be said to account for different portions of the print awareness test variance. The overlapping areas in Part A represent the amount of print awareness test variance that is explained by each of the background variables. In this case, each variable accounts independently for a significant proportion of variance in print awareness. To predict print awareness development, it appears necessary to know about both the amount of parents' education and the number of books available. The multiple correlation (R) of these two variables with print awareness is 0.71, substantially higher than the independent contributions of either of the separate variables to the explanation of performance on the print awareness test.

It is hard to believe, however, that there would be no relationship or overlap between amount of parents' education and number of available books. Well-educated parents probably own more books than do poorly educated parents. If the relationship of these background variables was perfect (correlation of 1.00), then neither of these variables would contribute any additional explanation of print awareness than that provided by either of them alone (see Figure 8–1, Part B). The multiple correlation of these

Figure 8–1
Three diagrams of shared variance between two background variables and print awareness

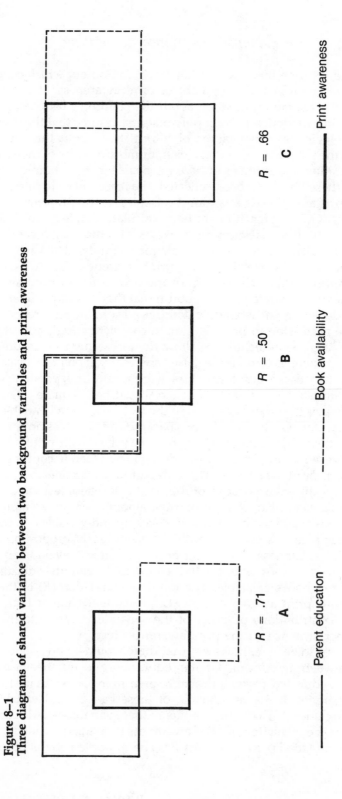

$R = .71$
A

$R = .50$
B

$R = .66$
C

———— Parent education

--------- Book availability

———— Print awareness

Note: The correlations of each of the background variables with the print awareness scores are equal in all cases ($r = .50$).

variables would be no higher than the simple correlation of either of them with the dependent measure, 0.50 in this case. For this reason, the removal of either of the background variables in Part B would not lead to any decrease in the size of the overlapping area.

The actual amount of overlap between the two independent measures is probably somewhere between the correlation limits of 0.00 and 1.00. Figure 8–1, Part C illustrates one such possibility. In this diagram, the two background variables have a 0.50 correlation with print awareness. However, there is a 0.36 correlation between the two background variables. For this reason, there is an area shaded by all three variables, representing the portion of print awareness variance that is explainable by either of the background measures. Both variables contribute additional explanation of print awareness, beyond that which could be provided by either variable taken alone. The multiple correlation in this case is 0.66, somewhat higher than the correlations of either of the background variables with print awareness. Regression analysis is useful in situations such as the one illustrated in Part C because it measures the combined contributions of the independent variables accurately.

Correlation (r) and multiple correlation (R) are conceptually identical. Nevertheless, because of the computational complications that arise through the use of more than two variables, r and R are not entirely analogous. Correlation coefficients can range from -1.00 to $+1.00$. This aspect of the statistic is useful because it shows both the magnitude and the direction of the relationship. R only ranges from 0.00 to $+1.00$, however. Multiple correlation coefficients only indicate the magnitude of relationship. Other multivariate statistics, discussed later in this chapter, must be examined to assess directionality.

Prediction and Explanation

Phrases such as *predicted variance, variance accounted for,* and *variance explained* abound in multivariate research studies. For example:

> Neither changing the order of the sentences nor giving the students a cloze passage on an unfamiliar topic lowered the scores. Multiple regressions performed on the passages showed little overall *variance explained* by the five *predictors.* (Leys, Fielding, Herman, and Pearson 1983, 113)

Or, from a recent study of vocabulary knowledge and comprehension by Freebody and Anderson (1983):

> Two way interactions not included in Table 3 *accounted* for nil variance. . . . The passage variable was *associated* with a significant proportion of the variance, as

in Experiment 1. . . . [The] verbal ability of the students and the particular passage used are strong *predictors.* (1983, 30)

These terms often appear to be used interchangeably, although they do not have precisely the same meanings. To explain what these terms mean and why researchers use them, it is necessary again to consider the meanings of correlation and causation (chapter 3).

Correlation refers to the extent to which two variables are interrelated. The measurement of the magnitude of such a relationship results in a correlation coefficient (r). Such coefficients are a useful index for comparing relationships. For example, Horn (1969) reports that spelling achievement and reading achievement are more closely related than are reading achievement and IQ for first-graders. The correlation coefficient can also be used to enter a significance table in order to ascertain whether two variables are related at levels beyond that which might be expected to occur by chance.

Researchers often attempt to infer a causal relationship between two variables on the basis of a correlation (Cook and Campbell 1979). As we discussed in chapter 3, this is frequently not a tenable inference because there are intervening or underlying variables that might be the actual source of the relationship. Nevertheless, let's assume a causal relationship between the linguistic complexity of books read aloud by parents to their children and the children's stages of language development. That is, we are assuming that the significant correlation of 0.33 between these variables, as reported by Chomsky (1972), indicates that parent reading behaviors cause some significant change in the syntactic complexity of children's oral language. How much change in children's oral language could we expect to find if we could induce parents to read more complex books to their children? The correlation coefficient does not directly answer this question.

Another statistic, the *coefficient of determination,* is needed in order to answer the question of how much change in one variable we can expect to find as a result of a change in another variable. The coefficient of determination is easily derived by squaring the correlation coefficient. In this case, the coefficient of determination (r^2) is 0.11. Thus, if we were able to get rid of or reduce *all of the variance in the parent book selection variable,* we could only expect to reduce the variability of their children's language development by 11 percent. Programs might be established to train all parents to read only high-level books to their children, but such efforts alone would be expected to increase the oral language development of their children by only about 11 percent. The coefficient of determination (r^2) can be interpreted as a proportion, while the correlation coefficient (r) cannot.

The descriptions and distinctions of r and r^2 are equally correct for R (multiple correlation) and R^2 (multivariate coefficient of determination). Thus, in the examples given in Figure 8–1, the R^2's are 0.50, 0.25, and 0.44, respectively. These statistics indicate how much change in print awareness test performance we might expect to cause if we were able to control both parents' education and number of books in the home, assuming, of course, a causal relationship between these variables and print awareness.

R^2 or r^2 are the statistics being referred to when researchers use the terms *variance accounted for, predicted variance,* and *variance explained*. Prediction means that we are able to infer scores on the dependent variable by knowing the values of the independent variables. In the case of the Chomsky data, we could state that the parent reading variable predicts 11 percent of the variance in children's language development. This means that knowing which books the parents read to their children would allow us to predict their children's stages of language development 11 percent better than we could just by chance.

The ideas of prediction or accounting for variance entail no assumption of causation. Of course, if we were able to measure all the conditions that affect the dependent variable, we would expect to be able to predict the dependent variable perfectly. This is how prediction and causation are related. But it is possible to predict performance on the dependent measure, even if we do not know exactly which conditions caused the dependent measure. Some researchers, in an attempt to show that they are not assuming causation, are careful to use the terms *prediction* or *variance accounted for*, rather than the more causally loaded term *explanation*. However, as Kerlinger and Pedhazur (1973) have noted, researchers rarely use variables that they think are unimportant or incidental. Because of this, the distinction between prediction and explanation in a nonexperimental study is not always clearly drawn.

Researchers are usually interested in more than just accurate predictions, even when conditions allow them to do no more than this. Researchers want to *explain* why things are as they are: Why some children read better than others, why children include certain types of information when they write stories, and the like. For this reason, researchers construct models or sets of independent variables on the basis of theories or implicit assumptions about how these things occur. These models then are used to explain, account for, or predict the variance in the data the researcher is attempting to understand. Often, the assumption of the researcher is that these variables will provide a meaningful causal explanation of literacy or language development. If the R^2 is of sufficient magnitude, the model will reveal which variables need to be manipulated in order to stimulate language or literacy learning. Although the term *variance explanation* does carry the implication of causal relationship, remember that the causal nature of the relationship is most often *inferred* but not *proven*.

Models and Variables

Multiple regression analysis allows the researcher to examine the effects of an entire constellation of independent variables simultaneously. It also permits the evaluation of the influence of a single independent variable *within the context of such a constellation*. To do either of these, the researcher must construct a model of the phenomenon to be explained. Such a model might show how the reading or writing process functions by describing the functional relationships between all or many of the essential parts in those processes. The regression analysis constructs a mathematical equation that shows how each of the independent variables must be weighted so that they combine for the best prediction of scores on the dependent variable.

In order to construct such complex models, the researcher relies on theory as well as information gleaned from previous empirical investigations. DeSoto and DeSoto (1983) noted the large numbers of research studies that linked reading comprehension with verbal processing abilities. Although the studies they reviewed did agree about the importance of verbal processing to reading achievement, they employed a diverse collection of verbal processing measures. In fact, this collection was so diverse that DeSoto and DeSoto concluded that these tests were not necessarily measuring identical verbal processing constructs.

> The present study was designed to evaluate the relationship between reading achievement and a number of diverse verbal processing abilities, . . . measures of memory span, associative learning, semantic association, automatic word processing, and time taken to name pictures, read words, and recode (pronounce) pseudowords. (1983, 118)

For this reason, DeSoto and DeSoto regressed a measure of reading comprehension on these ten measures of verbal processing. This regression accounted for 61 percent of the variance in reading comprehension—significantly more than was captured by any of the individual variables. This finding is of interest because it shows reading comprehension to be based on verbal processing to a greater degree than reported in previous studies. Moreover, it demonstrated that these verbal processing tests were measuring aspects of verbal processing that were somewhat separate and distinct.

DeSoto and DeSoto were not just interested in the total amount of variance in reading comprehension that could be accounted for, however. They also wanted to know something about the relative importance of each of the verbal-processing measures. There are a number of ways that the importance of the individual variables can be evaluated. One possibility is to examine the individual correlation coefficients of each of the verbal-processing variables with the reading-comprehension measure. In this case, all but one of the variables was found to be significantly correlated with reading comprehension (see Table 8-1).

Another way to measure the importance of the individual variables is to use multiple regression to find out how much of an increase in variance accounted for is associated with each measure. Care must be exercised in

Table 8–1
Intercorrelations between processing measures and reading comprehension for all 134 subjects

Variable	2	3	4	5	6	7	8	9	10	11
1. Visual Attention Span for Objects	51	46	36	-35	27	-25	-29	-38	00	39
2. Auditory Attention Span for Unrelated Words		60	39	-25	30	-30	-24	-30	-01	36
3. Auditory Attention Span for Related Syllables (sentences)			55	-30	36	-29	-27	-27	-04	49
4. Verbal Opposites				-35	55	-51	-48	-43	10	71
5. Van Wagenen Word Learning Test					-16	14	06	16	06	-39
6. Recoding Accuracy						-63	-63	-37	13	60
7. Recoding Time							58	38	-12	-53
8. Reading Words (time)								52	-18	-48
9. Picture Naming (time)									-22	-43
10. Automatic Word Processing (time)										03
11. Reading Comprehension										

Note: Decimal points have been omitted. For $r \geq .22$, $p < .01$; for $r \geq .17$, $p < .05$.
Source: J. L. DeSoto and C. B. DeSoto, Relationship of reading achievement to verbal processing abilities, *Journal of Educational Psychology* 75 (1983): 120. Copyright 1983 by the American Psychological Association. Reprinted by permission of the publisher and author.

interpreting such analyses, however, because the sequence in which variables are entered into the regression will influence the amount of variance that can be associated with each. In Figure 8–1, Parts B and C, it is clear that the variable used first in the regression will appear most important. In Part B, the variable used first will capture *all* of the accountable variance in the dependent measure. The second variable will not add any explanation because of its perfect correlation with the first independent measure. The interpretation would be that the first variable was important, but the second was not. Similarly, in Part C the independent variable specified first will capture 25 percent of the variance in the dependent measure, while the variable entered second will account for only 19 percent of the variance. In this case, the second dependent measure, if it had been used first, also would have captured the largest portion of the variance.

Order of Variable Entry

Because sequence of entry can influence the estimate of the relative importance of the independent variables, if there is a clear sequence of events, it is best to enter variables in the order in which they usually occur. For example, a researcher wants to know the relative impact of several variables (intelligence, language development, socioeconomic status, race, and school quality) on academic achievement. It is doubtful that the researcher would enter school quality first, simply because the students' contact with school comes so much later in time than their contact with the other variables.

In those cases in which an objectively well-ordered sequence of occurrence is not apparent, it is best to use theory to specify entry order. According to Piagetian theory, for example, language development follows cognitive development; thus, intelligence would be entered prior to language development. By entering intelligence first, the variance of the dependent measure is reduced to a level that would be expected if all of the subjects were equal in intelligence. The correlations of the variables entered into the regression subsequently are called *semipartial correlations*, because the effects of other variables have been statistically controlled or partialled out of the dependent measure. These semipartial correlations are squared in order to find out how much additional variance explanation is accomplished, given the variables already used in the analysis.

There are also, however, nontheoretical approaches to entry order. These procedures are referred to as *stepwise regressions*. DeSoto and DeSoto (1983) used a stepwise solution in their analysis of the relationship. A forward stepwise regression selects the independent variable most correlated with the dependent measure. Next, it selects the independent measure that adds the most additional significant explanation of the dependent measure. This process continues until either all of the variables have been entered or none of the available measures are able to account for additional significant portions of variance.

A stepwise multiple-regression analysis was performed to determine the variables that would together best account for Reading Comprehension. In this analysis the variable with the largest correlation with the remaining variance in Reading Comprehension was entered into the regression equation at each step. . . . Three variables entered the equation before non-significant improvement in explained variance was reached. . . . After this third step, none of the remaining variables, including the memory span measures, accounted for a significant amount of the residual variance in Reading Comprehension. (1983, 122)

In the DeSoto and DeSoto analysis, the Verbal Opposites measure entered first because of its high correlation with comprehension (see Table 8–2). The second variable associated with a significant amount of variance, given that the Verbal Opposites test was already in the regression, was the Recoding Accuracy measure. The third and final variable to enter this regression was the Word Learning test. Although the other seven measures together accounted for an additional 3 percent of the variance in reading comprehension, none of them alone was able to account for a significant

Table 8–2
Stepwise multiple regression on reading comprehension

Step entered	Variable	R^2	Increase in R^2
1	Verbal Opposites	.498	.498[a]
2	Recoding Accuracy	.560	.062[a]
3	Van Wagenen Word Learning Test	.587	.027[b]
4	Picture Naming (time)	.596	.009
5	Recoding Time	.602	.006
6	Auditory Attention Span for Related Syllables (sentences)	.608	.005
7	Automatic Word Processing (time)	.611	.003
8	Visual Attention Span for Objects	.613	.002
9	Auditory Attention Span for Unrelated Words	.614	.001
10	Reading Words (time)	.614	.000

[a] $p < .01$
[b] $p < .001$

Source: J. L. DeSoto and C. B. DeSoto, Relationship of reading achievement to verbal processing abilities, *Journal of Educational Psychology* 75 (1983): 120. Copyright 1983 by the American Psychological Association. Reprinted by permission of the publisher and author.

amount of comprehension variance. Table 8–2 indicates the amount of reading comprehension variation associated with each of the verbal-processing variables, given that the variables appearing above each in the table had already entered the regression. Note that of the three variables that would be rated as most important on the basis of the correlation coefficients (see Table 8–1), only one is important, considering the semipartial correlations (see Table 8–2). This is because those verbal-processing variables most related to comprehension are highly interrelated with each other. They account for little unique variance in reading comprehension.

Stepwise solutions tend to be misleading because they capitalize on chance. They are constructed on the basis of the relationships of variables *for a given sample of subjects,* rather than on any kind of theoretical understanding of the processes being explicated. Because relationships might be enhanced or attenuated for a given sample of subjects, the importance of the relative individual variables might be misjudged. For this reason, the replication of stepwise results is especially useful.

Tests of Significance

It is possible, in a study like DeSoto and DeSoto's, to measure the significance of the entire model or of each of the relationships measured by semipartial correlations. The F statistic is used for both purposes. DeSoto and DeSoto found that only three independent measures contributed significantly to the explanation of reading comprehension. For this reason, they tested the significance of their model with only three independent measures:

> Together these three variables . . . accounted for 58.7%
> of the variance of Reading Comprehension, F (3,130)
> = 61.59, $p < .001$. (1983, 122)

They found that these three variables taken together allowed for an estimation of reading comprehension scores so accurate that it might be expected to occur by chance less than 1 out of 1,000 times. The numbers 3 and 130 are degrees of freedom for the F statistic in this case. These numbers indicate the number of independent variables used in the regression (3) and the number of subjects minus the number of independent variables minus one ($134 - 3 - 1$).

DeSoto and DeSoto also conducted separate regressions on achieving and nonachieving readers in order to determine whether there were different patterns of results for the two groups. In these analyses, they were interested in the amounts of variance accounted for by each step, rather than by the entire model:

> Stepwise multiple-regression analyses were also conducted separately on each group of readers. The re-

sults differed from the above analysis, which was performed on the whole range of reading achievement scores. For the achieving reader group, Verbal Opposites was the first variable entered into the equation, accounting for 26.7% of the variance in Reading Comprehension, $F(1,65) = 23.65$, $p < .001$. (1983, 122–23)

The degrees of freedom for measuring the significance of the increase of R^2 associated with a given independent variable are slightly different than those used for testing the complete model. With individual variables, the first degree of freedom is equal to the number of independent variables used at that step (1). The second degree of freedom is equal to the number of subjects (67) minus the total number of independent variables used up to that step (1) minus 1.

In addition to the squared semipartial correlation statistic and its associated F, analyses of the individual variables sometimes report b weights (or β). These numbers are used to weight each variable in the regression equation according to its relative importance within the model.

The b weights are useful for comparisons of variables within the regression equation, rather than across equations. The b weights, like semipartial correlations, tend to be unreliable across models; that is, the b weights can change as a result of adding some other variable to the model. Sometimes comparisons of the importance of individual variables across different models is what the researcher wants to examine. Such comparisons should employ semipartial correlations, rather than b weights, because b weights do not operate within a well-specified range of values, such as 0.00 to 1.00, as do the semipartial correlations.

Freebody and Anderson (1983) report b weights in a study that assessed the relationship of a general standardized comprehension test with a number of specific measures of text comprehension. They reported b weights of 1.24 for recall score, 0.30 for detail recognition, 0.37 for main-idea recognition, and 0.68 for total recognition. These weights indicate that, for instance, reading ability, as measured by a particular standardized test, is more closely related to the recall measure than to the total recognition score. In fact, the reading test performance explains 39 percent of the recall score and only 21 percent of the recognition score.

Even when the relative explanation provided by a variable is stable across models, its b weight might change greatly. The b weights can be used to indicate whether a variable is exerting a positive or negative influence on the dependent measure. All of the relationships Freebody and Anderson studied were positive, as indicated by the b weights. This is useful information because the R's and R^2's are always 0.00–1.00, even if the variables have a negative relationship with the dependent measure. The R^2 of reading ability with total recall in this study is 0.39. That indicates the size of the relationship, but it does not indicate whether the recall scores are higher for low-ability or high-ability students. That b is $+1.24$ and not -1.24 indicates that one score rises along with the other.

Experiments, Quasi-Experiments, and Nonexperiments

Multiple regression can be used in analyzing data from experiments, quasi-experiments, and nonexperiments. An experiment is an attempt to determine causation through the manipulation of independent variables, while exercising direct control of extraneous influences upon the dependent measure. Because it is virtually impossible to exercise complete control over all possible extraneous variables in most reading and writing research, true experiments are rare. For this reason, it is difficult, if not impossible, to provide examples of the use of multiple regression with this type of reading and writing research.

Quasi-experiments are widely used in reading and writing research; they also determine causal outcomes of some manipulation. However, quasi-experiments use randomization and statistical control in addition to direct control to avoid the effects of misleading influences. Pflaum and Pascarella (1980), for example, assigned learning-disabled students to a control group or to one of three experimental groups. The experimental groups received various types of context-usage training. The provision or withholding of this training was the manipulation of interest. Pflaum and Pascarella directly controlled for the effects of amount of instruction by providing equal amounts of instruction to all of the groups. It is certain, therefore, that the finding that context training enhanced reading achievement for those with reading levels at second grade or above was not a result of the amount of teaching.

This study was unable to control directly for all variables that might have affected the outcomes. For this reason, subjects were randomly assigned to treatment groups. Randomization does not control the extraneous influences, but it balances such influences among groups. This balancing should equalize the impacts of the extraneous variables. If these subjects differed in IQ, randomization should lead to equal effects due to IQ for all groups, no matter which treatment was provided.

In addition to randomization, quasi-experiments employ statistical control of outside influences. *Statistical control* means that variation in the dependent measure related to the extraneous variable is reduced. In a regression, this means that the dependent measure is regressed first on the control variables, and then on the manipulated variables. Such an analysis is commonly referred to as an analysis of covariance because it controls the *covariance*, the variance shared by the dependent measure and the extraneous variables. Thus, variables that enter later in the regression can account only for variation that is not associated with the extraneous conditions. Pflaum and Pascarella controlled statistically for differences in prior reading achievement.

In regression analyses of quasi-experiments, the F statistic for the treatment-manipulation variable indicates whether the variable is significantly related to the dependent measure. The R^2 for this variable indicates the effect size, which tells how much influence the independent variable had on the outcome measure. The $R^2 = 0.17$ reported in the Pflaum and Pascarella study indicates that about 17 percent of the variation in post-treatment reading scores was due to the treatment.

A number of reading and writing studies have employed multiple regression with quasi-experimental designs. Shanahan, Kamil, and Tobin (1982) used regression to measure the influence of passage organization on cloze test performance. This quasi-experiment showed cloze to be insensitive to comprehension of information across sentences, even with the influence of prior knowledge controlled. Geva (1983), in an instructional study that used regression, found flowcharting to be an effective method for teaching comprehension. In another quasi-experiment that used regression, Reynolds and Anderson (1982) found attentional allocation differences for text information due to the availability of inserted questions; subjects spent greater time reading text information that had been cued by teacher-provided prereading questions.

Researchers also use regression to make causal inferences about non-manipulated variation. For example, Scribner and Cole (1981) wanted to determine the influence of literacy learning (both reading and writing) upon the cognitive development of individuals in a West African society. Of course, it would be unethical to withhold literacy teaching from subjects in order to measure the impact of such learning using an experimental or quasi-experimental approach. Scribner and Cole found it necessary to examine the abilities of existing groups of literates and nonliterates. Their regressions of this data led them to conclude that the ways that reading and writing are taught and used in society determine the impact of literacy on memory, deductive thinking, and other cognitive abilities. It could be argued that Scribner and Cole found relationships between literacy and cognition, but that they did not actually determine whether it was literacy or cognition that was the influential variable. Thus, it might be differences in cognition that lead individuals to learn and use literacy in different ways. It is also possible that the differences in cognition found in this study were due to other factors. Scribner and Cole attempted to control for the influence of several other factors and to build a strong theoretical explanation of their findings to overcome these limitations.

Researchers sometimes take a nonexperimental approach to causal questions simply because it would be difficult to manipulate the independent variable of interest. For example, Beebe (1980) attempted to determine the relative influences upon comprehension of various types of oral reading miscues. Subjects were asked to do oral reading, and the naturally occurring variations in their miscues were tabulated. Of the categories of miscues examined, only syntactically-semantically unacceptable miscues were found to be negatively related to comprehension. Self-corrections, although counted as errors in some systems of oral reading evaluation, actually were found to be positively related to comprehension. Obviously, any attempt to change these children's miscues would have led to an artificiality that would have limited the study's ecological validity. But the data analysis in a nonexperimental study can only specify the relationships. It is always possible that the direction of any relationship in such studies is different than the researcher has assumed, and that underlying, unspecified mechanisms are actually responsible for the relationship. Such criticism is appropriate for all nonexperimental regression research, including Evanechko, Ollila, and Armstrong's (1974) study of the reading-writing relationship and Leinhardt, Zigmond, and Cooley's (1981) study of the effects of various aspects of reading instruction.

All of these research approaches—experimental, quasi-experimental, and nonexperimental—are useful for *inferring* causation. Likewise, all of these research approaches can use multiple regression in an appropriate manner. Remember, however, that the statistical techniques do not determine the strength of the causal inferences that can be drawn. More important, in this regard, is the conceptualization of the research problem. Generally, for equally well-conceptualized studies of most reading and writing issues, manipulation and control will raise doubts about ecological validity, while nonexperimentation leads to questions of direct effect and directionality. Converging results of data analysis must be used in conjunction with theory to resolve such issues.

RECOGNIZING AND READING REGRESSION STUDIES

It is easy to recognize a regression study because the researcher will indicate the type of data analysis used in either the Methods or Results section of the study. If the researcher indicates that a given study employed multiple regression, you should try to answer the following questions. These questions, with slight changes, can be used with other forms of multivariate research, as well.

Questions for Regression Studies

This part of the chapter poses six questions for Hiebert, Englert, and Brennan's (1983) multiple regression study of expository text knowledge in reading and writing.

> This study investigated college students' awareness of different text structures in reading and writing ex-

pository material. In examining this awareness, the study had three aims. The first was to determine performance on different text structures when reading and writing expository text. The second aim was to examine the relationship of these performances to achievement on a general comprehension measure. The third aim was to compare performance on reading and writing tasks. (1983, 64)

Is the study an experiment, quasi experiment, or nonexperiment?

To answer this question, examine carefully the descriptions of the measures and procedures in the Methods section of the study. First, it is necessary to find out whether some manipulation or treatment is planned. If there is to be a manipulation, then the study is either an experiment or a quasi-experiment. If the independent variables of interest are not going to be altered, then it is a nonexperimental investigation.

If it is some form of experiment, it is necessary to ascertain whether the researcher is going to use direct control of extraneous variables or is relying on statistical controls and randomization. If only direct controls are being used, it is an experiment, while the use of statistical controls and randomization indicate that it is a quasi experiment.

In the Hiebert, Englert, and Brennan study, special instruments were designed in order to measure student knowledge of four expository text structures (description, sequence, enumeration, and comparison-contrast).

Twelve items also were developed for the writing test, with three items each for the four text structures. Each item presented students with the topic sentence of a paragraph. The same criteria were applied to the construction of these topic sentences as to the topic sentences used in the reading instrument. That is, topic sentences (a) indicated the topic of the paragraphs, and (b) signaled a specific type of text structure. In contrast to the reading measure, however, the writing measure required students to generate related details rather than to recognize related details. (1983, 69)

Clearly, these subjects were required to complete a series of specially designed reading and writing tests. Each text structure represented a different manipulation. Thus, this is either an experimental or a quasi-experimental study, because the independent variables (that is, the text structure conditions) are being manipulated.

These authors go on to describe how extraneous variables (such as order of presentation) were dealt with:

> Order effects were controlled [in this way]. . . . [T]est
> items were randomly distributed by first blocking on
> the four types of text structure, then randomly as-
> signing an item from each of the blocks to every set
> of four problems to ensure that every text structure
> was represented at least once in every set of four
> problems. (1983, 69)

Thus, order effects were controlled through random assignment of
items to positions. This study is therefore a quasi-experiment. An experimental study would have made certain that every subject saw items of each
type in each position. This study, instead, ensured that the items had an
equal probability of being read in each position. The randomization used
here seems reasonable given the number of passages used (there are more
than 479 million possible orders for 12 items).

We recommend that, when reading experiments or quasi-experiments
that use multivariate statistics, the reader ask the relevant questions from
this chapter and from the chapter on experiments (chapter 6). For nonexperiments that use multivariate analyses, use the questions from both this
chapter and the descriptive research chapter (chapter 4).

Is the model complete?
Are the variables in the proper order?

The characteristics of the model must be considered carefully. The
reader has to evaluate the model in terms of whether or not all relevant
variables are considered. The failure to include an important variable can
alter greatly the nature of the results. Such omissions can make some trivial
variables appear to have importance.

It is also necessary to consider the order in which the variables were
entered into the regression if semipartial correlations are provided. It is
possible that regression results will suggest a given variable is important
or trivial on the basis of entry order alone. The researcher should either
make a strong theoretical case for the entry order used, or alternative
regressions should be performed and their results compared. The reader
of such studies has to consider whether other logical or theoretical sequences are reasonable. Such considerations are necessary in evaluating
the validity of regression findings.

Hiebert, Englert, and Brennan (1983) wanted to examine the separate
contributions of reading and writing text structure variables to the students'
performances on a standardized reading comprehension test. Specifically,
these researchers wanted to know if reading comprehension was influenced by the knowledge represented by their expository reading and writing variables.

[S]tudents' total scores across all text types on the reading and writing measures were entered as independent variables in a stepwise multiple regression with reading achievement as the dependent variable. . . . [S]tudent performance on the writing measure accounted for the largest amount of variance. Writing scores accounted for 25% of the variance associated with reading achievement. When the scores on the reading measure [the text structure measure] were also entered into the equation, 31% of the variance was explained, resulting in a significant total R^2. It is interesting to note that reading scores also accounted for a significant ($p < .01$) amount of the variance when entered first in the equation. However, the average unique variance increment explained by reading was only 17%. Thus, students' writing performance—measured in terms of their ability to generate sentences compatible with the prevailing text structure—was a better predictor of reading achievement than their ability to recognize details consistent with text structure. (1983, 75)

These researchers tested alternative models. They found that the reading and writing measures both added to the overall explanation of reading comprehension; they also found writing to be more closely correlated with the comprehension measure.

However, other variables might have been included in this model. How well would comprehension relate to these text structure variables if other measures, such as vocabulary knowledge, syntactic complexity, prior knowledge, and so on, had been entered first? The importance of text structure knowledge might have been dramatically reduced.

Is the sample size sufficient to ensure an adequate test of the model?

In order to evaluate the adequacy of sample size, the reader simply examines the ratio of subjects to independent measures. This ratio should be approximately 20:1 (Ahlgren and Walberg 1975). As fewer subjects per measure are used, the R^2 tends to increase. This increase may appear impressive, but it is due to measurement error, not to the power of the explanatory model. Results from studies with low subjects-to-measures ratios are suspect, as they have a tendency to be highly unreliable.

The Hiebert, Englert, and Brennan study had 52 subjects and two independent variables, a ratio of 26:1. This suggests that, given a reasonably representative sample of subjects, the $R^2 = 0.31$ obtained for this model is probably reliable.

Is the R² of the overall model significant and meaningful?

First, it is necessary to examine the F statistic for the overall model. If it is significant, the use of the model increases our ability to explain or predict values on the dependent measure, above what could be done simply on the basis of chance. However, the use of a large enough sample can guarantee that even a miniscule improvement in prediction will be significant. For this reason, if the findings are significant, we must examine the magnitude of the R^2. R^2 is unaffected by sample size. It is an indication of the power and accuracy of the model. The nearer to 1.00 the R^2 comes, the more meaningful are the results. For most educational questions, R^2's in the range of 0.70–0.80 are about as high as can be expected. (With a reasonable subjects-to-measures ratio, R cannot be higher than the reliabilities of the dependent measures.)

The information in Table 8–3 indicates that the overall model is significant when both variables are entered into the equation. Note that the $R^2 = 0.31$; this means that this much explanation of the comprehension results would be expected to occur by chance less than 1 out of 10,000 times. Also, note that the R^2 is not especially large. There is a great deal of unaccounted variance here. Thus, reading comprehension is only weakly related to text structure knowledge, even when it is measured through both reading and writing. The use of a more comprehensive model would probably give us a better indication of the importance of these text structure variables, although it is important to note that this finding is consistent with other reading-writing relationship studies (Shanahan 1984).

Are the R²'s of the individual variables significant and meaningful?

Again, it is necessary to examine the F statistics for the individual variables to find out if they add to the prediction of the dependent measure beyond chance levels. If they do, then we examine the partial correlation

Table 8–3
Results of multiple regression analysis

Step	Variable(s) Added to Equation	R^2	F Value	p
1.	Writing	0.25	16.55	< .0001
2.	Reading and Writing	0.31	11.00	< .0001

Source: Hiebert, Englert, and Brennan 1983, 75. Used with permission of the National Reading Conference.

coefficients to find out whether these variables are sufficiently related to the dependent measure to be meaningful or important. How much change in the dependent variable can be effected by a change in the independent variable?

Table 8–3 indicates that the R^2 for the overall model (0.31) is significant. It does not indicate whether the increment in the R^2, 0.06, brought about by stepping in the reading variable, is significant. It is possible that these two variables actually fail to account for separate portions of the reading comprehension variance. The 6 percent increase in explanation brought about by the reading variable might not be significant.

It is also necessary to examine the correlations of each of these variables with the dependent measure or the b weights in order to ascertain directionality. Directionality will indicate what kind of change to expect in the dependent measure, given an increase or decrease in the value of the independent measure. For example, if amount of writing and writing achievement were positively related, then an increase in amount of writing would be expected to lead to an increase in writing achievement. If the correlation, or the b weights, for amount of writing was negative, then we would expect increases in amount of writing to lead to decreases in achievement.

The Hiebert, Englert, and Brennan study reported no b weights. But it did provide this information:

> An analysis to determine the relationship between the total scores across all text structures on the reading and writing measures indicated that the correlation between the two measures was significant ($r = .35$, $p < .01$). Additionally, the correlations between the reading and writing measures proved to be significant for three of the four text structures, including sequence ($r = .27$, $p < .05$), comparison-contrast ($r = .31$, $p < .05$), and enumeration ($r = .31$, $p < .01$). (1983, 75)

This indicates that the text structure variables were positively related to reading comprehension and to each other. That is, those subjects with the most knowledge of expository text structures had higher scores on the reading comprehension measure.

Have the results been replicated?

Regressions examine the relationships of variables for a given sample. Regression statistics can be inflated because the equations are made to fit the specific sample used. The same equation would rarely be expected to fit another sample as well. For this reason, the researcher should use the regression equation with a second sample of subjects. When this is done, the R^2's will be expected to shrink. Sometimes they shrink so much that significance is lost. The amount of shrinkage provides a better understanding of the reliability of the findings. It indicates how generalizable the results of the study are. Generally, very large R^2's, or R^2's derived from very large representative samples, do not suffer great amounts of shrinkage. Hiebert, Englert, and Brennan did not replicate their study. It is reasonable to assume that if they had replicated it, the R^2 would have decreased in size. The magnitude of such a decline is impossible to estimate. However, given the limited size of this R^2, it is possible that a decrease would reduce the relationship below the level of statistical significance.

OTHER TYPES
OF MULTIVARIATE ANALYSIS

As noted at the beginning of this chapter, many types of multivariate analysis are used either for measuring relationships between dependent and independent measures or for reducing large sets of variables. Regression analysis has been discussed in detail. Now we will provide a brief discussion of three other forms of multivariate analysis. These descriptions will provide a conceptual explanation of the procedures, definitions of statistics unique to these analyses, and examples of studies that employ these techniques.

MANOVA and Discriminant Analysis

Multivariate analysis of variance (MANOVA) is a set of procedures useful for studying the relationships that exist between multiple independent variables (usually group membership) and multiple dependent measures. MANOVA is useful in those cases in which the researcher tries to find out if groups of subjects differ on a variety of interdependent measures. Mikulecky (1982), for example, wanted to compare the literacy demands placed upon various occupational groups. Literacy demands were represented by several measures, including amount of reading time required, level of difficulty, importance, scope, depth of the reading material, and material format. Because these literacy demand variables were thought to be conceptually and statistically interdependent, it was necessary to analyze them as a set, rather than comparing the groups on each dependent variable separately.

Mikulecky found that various occupational groups did differ in the literacy demands placed upon them; Wilks Lambda (λ) = 0.60237, F = 4.06, $p < 0.00001$. The F statistic indicates that the differences in the groups on this set of measures were significant. The Wilks Lambda statistic (λ) is equal to $1 - R^2$, so $R^2 = 0.39763$ for this analysis. Thus, occupational differences explain 38 percent of the variance in literacy demands. Studies that employ MANOVA should always provide either the λ statistic or R^2, so that it is possible to estimate the size of the effect. Remember, however, that because λ and R^2 are complementary statistics, the smaller the λ, the greater the influence of the independent variables.

Mikulecky found that these groups differed on the literacy demand variables. But which of the literacy demand variables distinguished the groups? To find out which variables combined together to account for the group distinctions, the researcher performs a discriminant analysis. Some researchers mistakenly attempt simply to compare the groups on each of the dependent measures individually. Although an examination of the univariate differences does provide some useful information, the approach is not recommended as a complete follow up to MANOVA because it ignores the overlaps that exist between the dependent measures. Discriminant analysis is used to identify which variables combine together to distinguish the groups.

Discriminant analysis calculates statistics called *discriminant function coefficients*. These coefficients are similar to b weights in a regression. Discriminant function coefficients indicate the relative importance of each of the variables in the analysis, and it is possible to test the significance of each using the χ^2 statistic (comparable to the F statistic in use). Mikulecky found that groups differed significantly on the scope and importance variables. Once these variables were used to distinguish groups, however, the other variables contributed no additional explanation.

MANOVA and discriminant analysis have been used to study many reading and writing issues. They have been used to study the instructional decisions made by reading teachers (Borko and Niles 1982); the influence of cohesive relationships in student writing upon teachers' ratings of the coherence of that writing (Tierney and Mosenthal 1983); the influence of dialect differences on a variety of oral reading behaviors (Simons and Johnson 1974); group differences in several word recognition abilities, including the use of graphic and contextual information (Leslie 1980), initial word learning (Kibby 1979), and identification of polysyllabic words (Cunningham 1980); the influence of types of comprehension instruction on question-answering behavior (Hansen 1981); and the relationship of print awareness with several intellectual, linguistic, and experiential variables (Hiebert 1980).

Factor Analysis

Another form of multivariate analysis is *principle components factor analysis*. This type of analysis is based on the idea that tests that measure the same construct will be highly related, while tests that measure different constructs will have low correlations with one another. By examining the patterns of interrelationship that exist among sets of measures, it is possible to identify the number and nature of constructs actually being measured.

What factor analysis does is weight the original variables so that they combine to explain unique portions of the variance represented by all of the original tests.

Factor analysis can be used to test hypotheses about the existence of certain hypothetical constructs. The researcher might develop sets of items or tests that he or she believes to be theoretically representative of the constructs of interest. By administering these tests to subjects and then factor-analyzing the results, it is possible to examine whether the results are consistent with the hypothesized constructs. For example, Lewis and Teale (1980) hypothesized that attitude toward reading was a multidimensional concept or construct. That is, they believed there were three independent components of reading attitude: individual development, utility, and enjoyment. To test the existence of these components, the researchers carefully constructed a 40-item attitude survey, including 13 or 14 items intended to assess each construct. These tests were then administered to 118 grade 8 and 97 grade 12 students. Lewis and Teale found that their attitude survey did separate into three factors, with individual items being most related to the predicted factors. This study provides partial empirical support for the existence of a multidimensional construct of reading attitude.

Factor analysis can be used in a more exploratory way in order to identify the factors underlying some extant collection of measures. In the DeSoto and DeSoto (1983) study discussed earlier, it was reported that three factors underlay the ten verbal processing tests. On the basis of the factor loadings (the correlations of the original tests with the newly constructed factors), these researchers decided that the factors were verbal coding speed, memory span, and verbal operations. Only the verbal coding speed and verbal operations factors were found to be related to comprehension.

Factor loadings should always be provided in factor-analytic studies. These loadings, reported in the form of a correlation matrix, show the amount of correlation between the factors and the original tests. Generally, the researcher looks for the two or three measures that have the highest correlations with the factors. These measures are then used to define the factors. Researchers can differ in their interpretations of the nature of a given factor. Readers need to examine the factor loadings carefully, rather than blindly accept the researcher's interpretation.

Researchers also should provide communality statistics for each of the original variables. Communality (h^2) indicates the proportion of variance in the original test that is accounted for by the factors, which shows the relative contribution of each variable to the overall factor solution. The h^2 statistic is comparable to an R^2 statistic derived from a regression of the original test on the combined set of factors.

Finally, the researcher should indicate the amount of variance explained (R^2) by each factor. This indicates the relative importance of each factor in accounting for the variance measured by the total test set. It is possible to identify a statistically significant factor that accounts for very little of the original test variance. For example, a study might identify two factors for a large set of writing measures, indicating that this collection of tests only measures two separate abilities. However, when the researcher uses regression to study the relationship of the two factors with the original tests, 0.81 and 0.04 are the R^2's produced. This indicates that Factor 1 is able to account for more than 80 percent of the variance in the entire set of measures. Factor 2, in this case, is a separate factor, but it only accounts for a trivial amount of the original performances. Factor 1 is clearly more important than Factor 2; this second factor might be too small to be of any practical interest.

Factor analysis has been used to examine the relationship of prior knowledge and reading comprehension (Langer and Nicolich 1980), as well as the relationship of reading achievement and social acceptance (Crook, Gillet, and Richards 1982). Factor analysis also has been used to determine types of leisure reading activity (Greaney 1980).

IN SUMMARY

This chapter has discussed multivariate research techniques. These techniques were described as useful for examining relationships between sets of variables in experimental or quasi-experimental studies and for simplifying large sets of variables. It is important to understand multivariate analysis because this method is beginning to replace other forms of statistical analysis (such as analysis of variance) in reading and writing research. We expect multivarate treatments to become increasingly evident because of their ability to analyze the complex relationships of large numbers of variables.

Multiple regression, probably the most widely used of the multivariate procedures, was described in detail. Less thorough discussions of factor analysis, multivariate analysis of variance, and discriminant analysis were presented also. Questions were provided in order to assist the reader in the evaluation of multivariate studies.

REFERENCES

Ahlgren, A., & Walberg, H. J. (1975). Generalized regression analysis. In D. J. Amick & H. J. Walberg (Eds.), *Introductory multivariate analysis* (pp. 8–52). Berkeley, CA: McCutchan.

Beebe, M. J. (1980). The effect of different types of substitution miscues on reading. *Reading Research Quarterly, 15*, 324–336.

Borko, H., & Niles, J. (1982). Factors contributing to teachers' judgements about students and decisions about grouping students for reading instruction. *Journal of Reading Behavior, 14*, 127–140.

Chomsky, C. (1972). Stages in language development and reading exposure. *Harvard Educational Review, 42*, 1–33.

Cook, T. D., & Campbell, D. T. (1979). *Quasi-experimentation*. Boston: Houghton Mifflin.

Crook, P. R., Gillet, J. W., & Richards, H. C. (1982). Teacher-rated reading achievement and social acceptance among elementary school children. *Journal of Reading Behavior, 14*, 191–195.

Cunningham, P. M. (1980). Applying a compare/contrast process to identifying polysyllabic words. *Journal of Reading Behavior, 12*, 213–223.

Davis, F. B. (1983). Fundamental factors of comprehension in reading. In L. M. Gentile, M. L. Kamil, & J. S. Blanchard (Eds.), *Reading research revisited* (pp. 238–246). Columbus, OH: Merrill.

DeSoto, J. L., & DeSoto, C. B. (1983). Relationship of reading achievement to verbal processing abilities. *Journal of Educational Psychology, 75*, 116–127.

Evanechko, P., Ollila, L., & Armstrong, R. (1974). An investigation of the relationships between children's performance in written language and their reading ability. *Research in the Teaching of English, 8*, 315–326.

Freebody, P., & Anderson, R. C. (1983). Effects on text comprehension of differing proportions and locations of difficult vocabulary. *Journal of Reading Behavior, 15*, 19–40.

Geva, E. (1983). Facilitating reading comprehension through flowcharting. *Reading Research Quarterly, 18*, 384–405.

Greaney, V. (1980). Factors related to amount and type of leisure time reading. *Reading Research Quarterly, 15*, 337–357.

Grobe, C. (1981). Syntactic maturity, mechanics, and vocabulary as predictors of quality ratings. *Research in the Teaching of English, 15*, 113–125.

Hansen, J. (1981). The effects of inference training and practice on young children's reading comprehension. *Reading Research Quarterly, 16*, 391–417.

Hiebert, E. H. (1980). The relationship of logical reasoning ability, oral language comprehension, and home experiences to preschool children's print awareness. *Journal of Reading Behavior, 12*, 313–324.

Hiebert, E. H., Englert, C. S., & Brennan, S. (1983). Awareness of text structure in recognition and production of expository discourse. *Journal of Reading Behavior, 15*, 63–79.

Horn, T. D. (1969). Spelling. In C. W. Harris (Ed.), *Encyclopedia of educational research* (4th ed., pp. 1287–1299). New York: Macmillan.

Jansky, J., & de Hirsch, K. (1972). *Preventing reading failure*. New York: Harper and Row.

Johnson, D. P., Toms-Bronowski, S., & Buss, R. R. (1983). A critique of Frederick B. Davis's study: Fundamental factors of comprehension in reading. *Reading research revisited* (pp. 247–256). Columbus, OH: Merrill.

Kerlinger, F. N., & Pedhazur, E. J. (1973). *Multiple regression in behavioral research*. New York: Holt, Rinehart and Winston.

Kibby, M. W. (1979). The effects of certain instructional conditions and response modes on initial word learning. *Reading Research Quarterly, 14*, 147–171.

Langer, J., & Nicolich, M. (1981). Prior knowledge and its relationship to comprehension. *Journal of Reading Behavior, 12*, 187–201.

Leinhardt, G., Zigmond, N., & Cooley, W. (1981). Reading instruction and its effects. *American Educational Research Journal, 18*, 343–361.

Leslie, L. (1980). The use of graphic and contextual information by average and below-average readers. *Journal of Reading Behavior, 12,* 139–149.

Lewis, R. & Teale, W. H. (1980). Another look at secondary school students' attitudes toward reading. *Journal of Reading Behavior, 12,* 187–201.

Leys, M., Fielding, L., Herman, P., & Pearson, P. D. (1983). Does cloze measure intersentence comprehension? A modified replication of Shanahan, Kamil, and Tobin. In J. A. Niles & L. A. Harris (Eds.), *Searches for meaning in reading/language processing and instruction* (Thirty-second Yearbook of the National Reading Conference, pp. 122–129). Rochester, NY: National Reading Conference.

Mikulecky, L. (1982). Job literacy: The relationship between school preparation and workplace actuality. *Reading Research Quarterly, 17,* 400–419.

Pflaum, S. W., & Pascarella, E. T. (1980). Interactive effects of prior reading achievement and training in context on the reading of learning-disabled children. *Reading Research Quarterly, 16,* 138–158.

Reynolds, R. E., & Anderson, R. C. (1982). Influence of questions on the allocation of attention during reading. *Journal of Educational Psychology, 74,* 623–632.

Scribner, S., & Cole, M. (1981). *The psychology of literacy.* Cambridge, MA: Harvard University Press.

Shanahan, T. (1984). Nature of the reading-writing relation: An exploratory multivariate analysis. *Journal of Educational Psychology, 76,* 466–477.

Shanahan, T., Kamil, M. L., & Tobin, A. W. (1982). Cloze as a measure of intersentential comprehension. *Reading Research Quarterly, 17,* 229–256.

Simons, H. D., & Johnson, K. R. (1974). Black English syntax and reading interference. *Research in the Teaching of English, 8,* 339–358.

Stewart, M. F., & Leaman, H. L. (1983). Teachers's writing assessments across the high school curriculum. *Research in the Teaching of English, 17,* 113–125.

Tierney, R. J., & Mosenthal, J. H. (1983). Cohesion and textual coherence. *Research in the Teaching of English, 17,* 215–230.

Walberg, H. J., & Shanahan, T. (1983). High school effects on individual students. *Educational Researcher, 12,* 4–9.

Witte, S. P., Daly, J. A., Faigley, L., & Koch, W. R. (1983). An instrument for reporting composition course and teacher effectiveness in college writing programs. *Research in the Teaching of English, 17,* 243–261.

Zaharias, J. A., & Mertz, M. P. (1983). Identifying and validating the constituents of literary response through a modification of the response preference measure. *Research in the Teaching of English, 17,* 231–242.

ADDITIONAL SOURCES
OF MULTIVARIATE RESEARCH PROCEDURES

Amick, D. J., & Walberg, H. J. (Eds.). (1975). *Introductory multivariate research.* Berkeley, CA: McCutchan.

Borg, W. R., & Gall, M. D. (1979). *Educational research: An introduction* (3rd ed.). New York: Longman.

Cronbach, L. J. (1975). Beyond the two disciplines of scientific psychology. *American Psychologist, 30,* 116–127.

Finn, J. D. (1974). *A general model for multivariate analysis.* New York: Holt, Rinehart and Winston.

Gorsuch, R. L. (1974). *Factor analysis.* Philadelphia: Saunders.

Kerlinger, F. N. (1973). *Foundations of behavioral research* (2nd ed.). New York: Holt, Rinehart and Winston.

Marzano, R. J. (1978). Path analysis and language research. *Research in the Teaching of English, 12,* 77–90.

Nunnally, J. C. (1967). *Psychometric theory.* New York: McGraw-Hill.

ADDITIONAL EXAMPLES
OF MULTIVARIATE STUDIES

Adams, A., Carnine, D., Gersten, R. (1982). Instructional strategies for studying content area texts in the intermediate grades. *Reading Research Quarterly, 18,* 27–55.

Carey, R. F., Harste, J. C., & Smith, S. L. (1981). Contextual constraints and discourse processes: A replication study. *Reading Research Quarterly, 16,* 201–212.

Cohen, S. G., Bridge, C. A., & Winograd, P. N. (1982). Semantic analysis of children's writing. In J. A. Niles & L. A. Harris (Eds.), *New inquiries in reading research and instruction* (Thirty-first Yearbook of the National Reading Conference, pp. 294–299). Rochester, NY: National Reading Conference.

Daly, J. A., & Wilson, D. A. (1983). Writing apprehension, self-esteem, and personality. *Research in the Teaching of English, 17,* 327–341.

Drum, P. A., Calfee, R. C., & Cook, L. K. (1981). The effects of surface structure variables on performance in reading comprehension tests. *Reading Research Quarterly, 16,* 486–514.

Gorrell, D. (1983). Toward determining a minimal competency entrance examination for freshman composition. *Research in the Teaching of English, 17,* 263–274.

Hare, V. C. (1982). Preassessment of topical knowledge: A validation and an extension. *Journal of Reading Behavior, 14,* 77–85.

Juel, C., & Holmes, B. (1981). Oral and silent reading of sentences. *Reading Research Quarterly, 16,* 545–568.

Langer, J. A. (1984). The effects of available information on responses to school writing tasks. *Research in the Teaching of English, 18,* 27–44.

Martinez, J. G. R., & Johnson, P. J. (1982). An analysis of reading proficiency and its relationship to complete and partial report performance. *Reading Research Quarterly, 18,* 105–122.

Meyer, B. J. F., Brandt, D. M., & Bluth, G. J. (1980). Use of top-level structure in text: Key for reading of ninth-grade students. *Reading Research Quarterly, 16,* 72–103.

Rentel, V., & King, M. (1983). Present at the beginning. In P. Mosenthal, L. Tamor, & S. A. Walmsley (Eds.), *Research on writing* (pp. 139–176). New York: Longman.

Chapter 9

Integrating and Summarizing Research Results

In the previous chapters, we have examined some of the major research methods, paradigms, and traditions. We have focussed on the understanding of different sorts of studies separately. In this chapter, we will address a common problem that consumers of research encounter: How does one make sense out of a series of studies that have reached disparate or contrary conclusions?

As you read a number of research studies, you may be left with the impression that researchers always disagree with each other. In fact, that *is* often the case. Researchers do not always study precisely the same problem. Even when they do, each researcher may study a different aspect of the problem. When studying a subject as complex as education, even the smallest difference in research procedures may translate into different findings.

Research is based on the notion that findings need to be verified. That is, when one researcher presents findings, they should be described in sufficient detail to allow others to verify or replicate them. For conclusions to be accepted, the research on which they are based should be replicated.

REPLICATION

Replication is, in its strict interpretation, performing the same research study again; the variables, methods, and conditions under which the original study was conducted should remain the same. Strictly speaking, there should be no variations. This is, of course, not entirely possible. Every time a study is performed, it has to be on a new sample or else on the same sample, which has been changed by the experiences of having participated in the experiment.

We do not generally hold replications to such strict criteria. So long as the variables and the general methodology are the same as the original, we are satisfied that the study qualifies as a replication. More commonly, replications include extensions of the original that make the interpretation more generalizable. Often, any quirks in the original may be cleaned up to eliminate confounding factors or other problems. In general, the more often a study is replicated with the same results, the more confidence one can have in those results.

When you begin searching for research to determine what sorts of instructional practices you might implement, be sure that you know the situation in which you want to do the implementation. Then you should search for studies that match your environment. For example, you may want to start a vocabulary improvement program in your suburban sixth-grade class that is achieving well above normal on standardized achievement tests. You should try to find research that has studied vocabulary for populations similar to yours.

If you are *really* lucky, you may find a study that has done just what you want to do. If so, examine the results to see whether it would be worth the effort to set up the new program. If not, look for something else. There are no hard rules about determining the value of implementing a program. However, consider this general rule: Most programs have to be in place for a long time (often two to three years) before tangible, lasting results can be realized.

Given the very large number of studies that have been done in reading, this search for a precise match may be an inefficient use of time. If, for example, you are looking for something to do with your sixth grade and read a study that has used fifth-grade students, what should you do? Or what about finding studies using adult students? Or those using remedial populations? If there are no studies to guide your choice of implementations, you may have to make do. Fortunately, there are usually some relevant studies, even if you have to make some inferences about the specific situation with which you are dealing.

The first step in translating research into practice is to *read the studies very carefully!* In the preceding sections of this volume, we presented questions that are important in understanding studies in each of the major research traditions. You should ask and answer each of these questions for each study you consider. There is no way to short-circuit or bypass this step if your goal is an accurate translation of research. Studies that are not well performed or that have ignored (usually unintentionally) important variables should have less influence on your decisions about instruction than studies that are tight, well done, and comprehensive. If you *cannot* answer some of the questions for a given study, you should not feel very confident about applying its findings. This does not necessarily mean that the study is invalid. It simply means that it cannot be accurately evaluated by generally accepted criteria. However, if a large enough number of flaws or unanswered questions exists, we may have to suspend judgment about the worth of the study. That is, even though we cannot assume the study is worthless, we must be *very* careful about believing the results.

Remember, the cumulative and progressive nature of scientific inquiry means that a study that seems near perfect today may be shown to have flaws when new information is uncovered in the future. A series of such examples can be found in Gentile, Kamil, and Blanchard (1983). This work is a collection of classic studies in reading, subjected to new analysis from contemporary perspectives. Keeping up with current research is a continuing job. New research often makes it important to rethink the conclusions reached about earlier findings.

Obviously, few people are able to keep up with the research in any more than a few areas. Thus, in order to facilitate making instructional implementation decisions when the alternatives are not so clear, we have to synthesize the research in the particular areas in which we are interested. We do not always have to do this for ourselves. We can search for research syntheses done by others. Such syntheses or research reviews can be conducted in several different ways, as provided by several sources.

LOCATING RESEARCH STUDIES AND REVIEWS

Before reading research, you have to be able to locate appropriate studies. Research studies are found primarily in journals. However, a recent trend is to include some research studies in books based on conference or symposium proceedings. Appendix A includes a list of journals that report research in reading and writing.

Typically, each journal includes a yearly index of relevant topics. Once you have located research by specific individuals, you can use that information to look for other articles by the same researchers. In addition, you can use the reference list with each article to determine whether there are other materials you should read.

More efficient procedures are available, including a number of indexing or abstracting services designed to provide faster and more organized access to research literature. Some of these are computerized to make searching even easier.

For educational research, one can consult *Resources in Education*, a monthly publication. It contains abstracts of reports, presentations at conferences, and other studies. It is a good source of material that is often unavailable elsewhere. *Psychological Abstracts* reviews about a thousand journals in psychology and related fields. Each monthly issue contains abstracts of journal articles, crosslisted by topic and author. While the emphasis is on psychological literature, much educational research literature is also included. A similar publication for education journals is the *Current Index to Journals in Education*, published monthly by Educational Resources Information Clearinghouse (ERIC).

Another important source is *Dissertation Abstracts*, which contains abstracts of dissertations, usually before they are published elsewhere. A more extensive list of these sources is contained in appendix A.

In most university libraries, some of these sources can be searched quickly and efficiently by computer. The user has to consult the *Thesaurus of ERIC Descriptors* to find key words to narrow the topic. When these descriptors are entered into the data base, a list of relevant studies is returned, often with abstracts. For sources that are not computerized, like *Psychological Abstracts*, a similar search can be done manually.

The search for reviews is similar. Among these are *Review of Educational Research*, *Review of Research in Education*, *Psychological Review*, and the *Summary of Investigations Relating to Reading*, published by the International Reading Association. Articles from these sources will also be listed and retrievable from ERIC.

An Example
of Locating Research Reviews

We will now follow an example of how one group of investigators used some common sources to locate information in which they were interested. Guthrie, Seifert, and Mosberg (1983) wanted to locate reading research reviews. Nonetheless, the procedure they used is a good illustration of how a search for reviews or original research studies should be conducted:

Locating Reviews of Research

Five literature banks were examined exhaustively to retrieve reviews of research on reading. These included Educational Resources Information Clearinghouse (ERIC, which began in 1966), Language and Language Behavior Abstracts (LLBA, 1973), Psychological Abstracts (PA, 1967), Social SciSearch (ISI, 1972), and Sociological Abstracts (SA, 1963). The descriptors that were employed to extract target articles included reading, comprehension, word meaning, literacy, text, prose, readability, vocabulary, linguistics, and disability or dyslexia. Some of the literature banks did not admit these descriptors but similar entries were used in those cases. In addition, the term review or literature review was used to locate articles. This search led to the identification of 214 articles which were classified as published reviews of research on some aspect of reading either by the author or a coder who entered it into a literature bank.

To locate books which were themselves reviews of research or contained chapters that reviewed research on reading, we used the subject guide to Books in Print for 1979–1980. The categories that we located and the accompanying numbers of books in each category were comprehension, 19; dyslexia, 26; illiteracy, 36; reading, 1,307. Books written by a single author in which the content was substantially a research synthesis were included. Edited volumes in which some of the chapters were research summaries were included. Books were not included if they were primarily oriented to testing, pedagogy, children's literature, practical guides in teacher education, or parents. After duplicates were eliminated from the set of retrieved books, a total of 128 books remained as our corpus. Each single-authored volume and each chapter of each edited book was examined to determine whether it was a review of research on reading. Finally, 22 single-authored volumes were identified, and 57 chapters from edited books were located. For both periodicals and books, the disciplines of social and behavioral sciences were included. Scholarship on reading issuing from the humanities such as literary criticism or philosophy was not included in the present investigation, despite its undeniable value for understanding reading.

As noted earlier, Guthrie et al. were interested in reviews. The procedure for locating single research studies does not differ significantly. What will differ in each search is the specific descriptors, which correspond to the topic of interest.

SYNTHESIZING AND USING RESEARCH

Three major techniques are used for synthesizing research: reviews, meta-analyses, and box scores or tallies. Most reviews and techniques for reviewing have been based on the experimental models of research. However, ethnographic research is often reported in qualitative rather than quantitative terms; that is, there are sometimes no numbers, statistics, or other quantifiable measures available for the calculations used in, for example, meta-analyses. Thus, some of the reviewing and synthesizing techniques discussed below are appropriate in only the experimental traditions of research. We will deal with each of these research synthesis techniques in turn.

Integrative Reviews

The goal of an *integrative review* is to collect all of the research done on a specific topic, subject each study to critical examination, and propose a comprehensive explanation that will cover all of the studies. The final explanation should also be able to account for any disparate findings, as well as those that are in agreement. Integrative reviews are distinguished from summative reviews, in which there is no attempt to do more than report what the findings are in a series of studies. Summative reviews can be helpful in locating information on specific topics, but they do not advance or synthesize findings.

Almost every research study has a review of prior research literature on the topic at hand. These reviews are also good places to search for relevant studies on the topic in which you are interested.

Questions for Integrative Reviews

Here are some questions that will help you determine the quality and, consequently, the usefulness of reviews:

1. Is the scope of the set of studies to be examined clearly spelled out? That is, are the variables of interest clearly defined? Are the problems precisely stated?

2. Are criteria for the inclusion of the studies clearly formulated and applied? Are only certain types of studies (correlational, experimental, ethnographic, and so on) included? Is there a rationale for the procedure?

3. Does the reviewer examine each study for its methodological soundness? Are studies then excluded on the basis of this examination? Are the criteria for methodological soundness specified?

4. Is an overall explanation proposed for the studies that remain? Does the explanation deal with the contrary results?

5. How comprehensive is the review? Where did the author of the review find the studies to review? Are the sources, journals, and the like clearly indicated? Is the review current? Does it cover older yet important studies? Have you run across studies that are not included?

These questions are related to the tasks suggested by Jackson (1980) as being critical for the production of competent integrative reviews. The consumer should ask these questions to be certain that the author of a review has followed rigorous procedures in his critique. These questions serve much the same function as the questions a consumer asks about a research study: They will guide the reader to the important dimensions on which to judge the worth of a review.

An Example

An illustration of an integrative review is the work of Sticht et al. (1974), who were interested in knowing whether oral language comprehension (auding) training transferred to reading comprehension. In other words, did oral language training facilitate reading comprehension? To study this problem, they developed four hypotheses:

1. Performance on measures of ability to comprehend language by auding will surpass performance on measures of ability to comprehend language by reading during the early years of schooling until the reading skill is learned, at which time the ability to comprehend by auding and reading will become equal.

2. Performance on measures of ability to comprehend language by auding will be predictive of performance on measures of ability to comprehend language by reading *after* the decoding skills of reading have been mastered.

3. Performance on measures of rate of auding and rate of reading will show comparable maximal rates of language and conceptualizing for both processes, assuming fully developed reading decoding skills.

4. Training comprehending by auding of a particular genre (e.g., "listening for the main idea") will transfer to reading when that skill is acquired. Conversely, once reading skill is acquired, new cognitive content learned by reading will be accessible by auding.

For this example, we will review the evidence on hypothesis 1. Tables 9–1 and 9–2 (from Sticht et al. 1974) show how the studies related to this hypothesis were analyzed along dimensions shown to be relevant in this line of research. The data from these tables are summarized in Figure 9–1 to reach a conclusion. The authors concluded that, based on the data from the tables and figure, the first hypothesis was supported. In a similar manner, the authors review and analyze other sets of studies to determine support for the remaining hypotheses.

Perhaps the only oversight in this review is that the authors do not

Table 9–1
Summary of research comparing auding and reading vocabulary

Grade Level	Subjects	Materials	Presentation Order	Controls Used			Results	Reference
				Auding, Reading Rates Matched	Reading Time Matched to Auding Time	Reading Time Not Specified		
1	Identical	Identical	Read first				A > R	Armstrong, H. C. 1953
2	Identical	Identical	Read first				A > R	Armstrong, H. C. 1953
	Identical	Identical	Aud first				A > R	Hauser, M. H. 1963
3	Identical	Identical	Read first				A > R	Armstrong, H. C. 1953
	Identical	Identical	Aud first				A > R	Hauser, M. H. 1963
	Identical	Identical	Counterbalanced				A > R	Miller, E. A. 1941
	Identical	Identical	Counterbalanced				A > R	Yates, P. S. 1937
4	Identical	Identical	Read first				A > R	Armstrong, H. C. 1953

Table 9–1 (continued)

	Identical	Identical	Counter-balanced	A > R	Miller, E. A. 1941
	Identical	Identical	Counter-balanced	A > R	Yates, P. S. 1937
5	Identical	Identical	Read first	A > R	Armstrong, H. C. 1953
	Identical	Identical	Counter-balanced	A = R	Yates, P. S. 1937
6	Identical	Identical	Read first	A > R	Armstrong, H. C. 1953
	Identical	Identical	Counter-balanced	A = R	Yates, P. S. 1937
7	Identical	Identical	Read first	A > R	Armstrong, H. C. 1953
12	Identical	Equivalent	—	R > A ✓	Burton, M. 1943

Table 9–1 (continued)

Grade Level	Subjects	Materials	Presentation Order	Controls Used — Auding, Reading Rates Matched	Reading Time Matched to Auding Time	Reading Time Not Specified	Results	Reference
College								
Low Reading Ability Subjects	Identical	Equivalent					A > R	Anderson, I. H. and Fairbanks, G. 1937
Median Reading Ability Subjects	Identical	Equivalent					R > A	Anderson, I. H. and Fairbanks, G. 1937
High Reading Ability Subjects	Identical	Equivalent					R > A	Anderson, I. H. and Fairbanks, G. 1937
	Identical	Equivalent		—	—	✓	A = R	Schubert, D. G. 1953

Source: Sticht et al. 1974, 74–75. Used with permission.

Table 9–2
Summary of research comparing auding and reading comprehension

Grade Level	Subjects	Materials	Presentation Order	Auding, Reading Rates Matched	Reading Time Matched to Auding Time	Reading Time Not Specified	Results	Reference
				Controls Used				
3	Identical	Identical	Counter-balanced				A > R	Erickson, C. I. and King, I. 1917
	Identical	Identical	Counter-balanced				A > R	Miller, E. A. 1941
4							A > R	Brassard, M. B. 1970
	Identical	Identical	Counter-balanced				A = R	Emslie, E. A., et al. 1954
	Identical	Identical	Counter-balanced				A > R	Erickson, C. I. and King, I. 1917
	Matched	Identical	N/A	—	✓	—	A > R	Hampleman, R. S. 1958
	Identical	Identical	Counter-balanced				A > R	Hanna, R. C. and Liberati, M. 1952

169

Table 9–2 (continued)

Grade Level	Subjects	Materials	Controls Used				Results	Reference
			Presentation Order	Auding, Reading Rates Matched	Reading Time Matched to Auding Time	Reading Time Not Specified		
	Identical	Identical	Counter-balanced				A > R	Joney, O. L. 1956
	Identical	Identical	Counter-balanced				A = R	Miller, E. A. 1941
	Identical	Equivalent	Counter-balanced	—	—	✓	A > R	Young, W. E. 1930
	Identical	Equivalent	Counter-balanced	—	✓	—	A > R	Young, W. E. 1930
5							A > R	Brassard, M. B. 1970
Measure of "Total Meaning"	Matched	Identical	N/A				A > R	England, D. W. 1952
Measure of "Retention of Details"	Matched	Identical	N/A				A = R	England, D. W. 1952

Table 9–2 (continued)

	Identical	Identical	Counter-balanced	—			A > R	Erickson, C. I. and King, I. 1917
	Matched	Identical	N/A	—	✓	—	A > R	Friedman, R. M. 1959
	Matched	Identical	N/A	✓	—	—	A > R	Russell, R. D. 1923
	Matched	Identical	N/A	—	✓	—	A > R	Russell, R. D. 1923
	Identical	Equivalent	Counter-balanced	—	✓	—	A > R	Young, W. E. 1930
	Identical	Equivalent	Counter-balanced	✓	—	—	A = R	Young, W. E. 1930
6	Identical	Identical	Counter-balanced	—			A > R	Brassard, M. B. 1970
	Matched	Identical	N/A	—	✓	—	A > R	Erickson, C. I. and King, I. 1917
	Identical	Identical	Counter-balanced	✓	—	—	A > R	Hampleman, R. S. 1958
	Identical	Identical	Counter-balanced	—	✓	—	A > R	Kelly, E. V. et al. 1952
Boys	Identical	Identical	Counter-balanced	—	✓	—	A > R	King, W. H. 1959
Girls	Identical	Identical	Counter-balanced	—	✓	—	A = R	King, W. H. 1959
	Identical	Equivalent	Counter-balanced	✓	—	—	A = R	Young, W. E. 1930

171

Table 9–2 (continued)

Grade Level	Subjects	Materials	Presentation Order	Auding, Reading Rates Matched	Reading Time Matched to Auding Time	Reading Time Not Specified	Results	Reference
	Identical	Equivalent	Counterbalanced	—	✓	—	A = R	Young, W. E. 1930
	Identical	Identical	Counterbalanced	—	✓	—	R > A	Many, W. A. 1965
7	Identical	Identical	Counterbalanced				A > R	Erickson, C. I. and King, I. 1917
	Identical	Identical	Counterbalanced				A = R	Kelly, E. V., et al. 1952
	Matched	Identical	N/A	—	✓	—	A = R	Russell, R. D. 1923
	Matched	Identical	N/A	—	—	✓	A = R	Russell, R. D. 1923
8	Identical	Identical	Counterbalanced				A > R	Erickson, C. I. and King, I. 1917

Controls Used

172

Table 9–2 (continued)

Grade	Groups	Materials	Procedure				Results	Study
9	Identical	Identical	Counter-balanced	—		—	A > R	Erickson, C. I. and King, I. 1917
	Matched	Identical	N/A	—	✓	—	A = R	Russell, R. D. 1923
	Matched	Identical	N/A	✓	—	—	A = R	Russell, R. D. 1923
11	Identical	Identical	Counter-balanced	—	✓	—	R > A	Haugh, O. M. 1952
College	Identical	Equivalent	—	—	✓	—	R > A	Brown, J. I. 1948
Poorest Readers	Identical	Identical	Counter-balanced		✓		A > R	Greene, E. B. 1934
Total Group Minus Poorest Readers	Identical	Identical	Counter-balanced				R > A	Greene, E. B. 1934
	Independent	Identical					R > A	Henneman, R. H. 1952
	Independent	Identical	N/A	—	✓	—	R > A	Jester, R. E. and Travers, R. M. W. 1966
	Independent	Identical	N/A	✓	—	—	A = R	King, D. J. 1968
	Identical	Equivalent	Counter-balanced	✓	—	—	R > A	Larsen, R. P. and Feder, D. D. 1940

Table 9–2 (continued)

Grade Level	Subjects	Materials	Presentation Order	Controls Used			Results	Reference
				Auding, Reading Rates Matched	Reading Time Matched to Auding Time	Reading Time Not Specified		
	Inde-pendent	Identical	N/A	—	—	✓	A > R	Worcester, D. A. 1925
Adults Low Aptitude Men	Identical	Identical	Counter-balanced	—	✓	—	A = R	Sticht, T. G. 1968
Average Aptitude Men	Identical	Identical	Counter-balanced	—	✓	—	A = R	Sticht, T. G. 1968
				—	✓	—	R > A	Webb, W. B. and Wallon, E. J. 1956
				—	—	✓	A = R	Webb, W. B. and Wallon, E. J. 1956
	Identical	Identical	Counter-balanced	✓	—	—	A > R	Goldstein, H. 1940

Source: Sticht et al. 1974, 76–81. Used with permission.

Figure 9–1
Comparison of auding and reading performance at five schooling levels

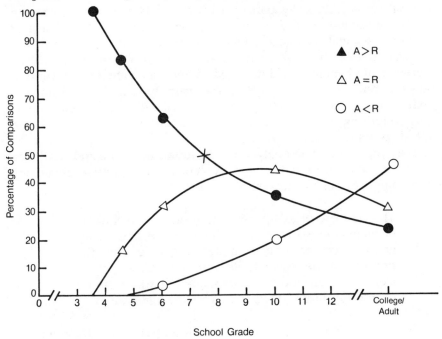

Source: Sticht et al. 1974, 82. Used with permission.

precisely indicate how they searched the literature for the studies they eventually considered. However, they do make this point:

> A hindrance to a comprehensive review of literature bearing on any one of these hypotheses is the large number of unpublished theses and dissertations of relevance, and the fact that many libraries will not provide inter-library loans of these materials. Since we could not obtain some studies, this review cannot be considered exhaustive. (Sticht et al. 1974, 72)

Thus, while validity might be threatened because of a biased or incomplete literature search, the authors have at least informed the reader to beware. Note, however, that we do not know whether the authors have found all of the relevant studies or not. (Remember, they did not obtain many unpublished studies.) What we do know is how they searched for those that they did find.

Meta-Analyses

A *meta-analysis* is technically part of a review. It is a way of combining results from a number of studies according to mathematical rules. The goal is to summarize, mathematically, what we know about the findings in a given research area. In a review or research synthesis, the author often has a great deal of subjective latitude. Meta-analysis removes some of that latitude and replaces it by estimating the magnitude and significance of research findings, based on results of studies already performed. This is done by weighting the value of each study according to its rigor and the magnitude of its findings.

An example of a meta-analysis can be found in Moore and Readence (1980). They were interested in the problem of how graphic organizers affect learning from text. They state:

> The purpose of this paper is to utilize the technique of meta-analysis to examine the effect of graphic organizers on learning from text. By integrating the findings of the research literature on graphic organizers, generalizations can be made regarding the research supporting their use as a teaching strategy.

They indicate how they searched for studies and how they decided to include specific pieces of research in their sample:

> The references that were consulted to identify research studies for this meta-analysis included *CIJE*, *Dissertation Abstracts*, *ERIC*, and bibliographies of the research documents themselves. In order to be included in this analysis, a research study needed to meet two criteria: 1) one of the experimental treatments had to include a graphic organizer as described by Barron (1969), and 2) sufficient statistical information had to be reported so that measures of association could be recovered.

The authors indicate how they analyzed the studies they located in the following passage:

> Measures of association were calculated by two methods. In the first method, *t* and *F* ratios were converted to point biserial (r_{pb}) and (η) values respectively, following equations specified by Cohen (1965). In the second method, with studies not reporting *t* or *F* ratios but reporting means and standard deviations, *d* values were calculated according to Glass (1976). These

d's, in turn, were transformed to r_{pb} values (Cohen, 1977). . . . If the control group or another treatment group produced means higher than the graphic organizer group, then the resulting measure of association was labelled negative and treated as such. Final, r_{pb} and values were each transformed to Fisher's Z' in order to treat them with descriptive statistics.

Moore and Readence go on to examine several variables, each time using a subset of the studies. For each of the questions they ask, they calculate the mean and median (and standard error, where appropriate) of the measures of association (correlations). We will examine two of these subanalyses:

Overall results of the combined studies indicate a small measure of association ($M = 15$; $SD = .21$; $SE = .02$; $Md = .11$) between treatment with a graphic organizer and subsequent learning from text. In fact only 2% of the variability in learning from text can be explained by knowing whether subjects were involved with graphic organizers or not. The rather large standard deviation indicates wide variability in the results. . . . Therefore, the median may be the better measure of central tendency for the overall findings.

After explaining that average performance may obscure individual variables, Moore and Readence examine several other aspects of the research:

Four studies investigated the construction of graphic organizers by the readers, themselves, as a post-reading activity. These studies obtained a large ($M = .39$; $Md = .38$). However, since only five measures of association are included here, this relatively large finding should be interpreted with care.

Cohen (1977) has suggested that the rule of thumb for interpreting measures of association should be that small values are approximately 0.10; medium values about 0.24; and large values are 0.37 and above. These are guidelines, not firm rules.

Moore and Readence conclude from their analysis, in part, the following:

Overall findings of this meta-analytic study reveal generally small effects of graphic organizers on learning from text. These findings preclude the unqualified use of graphic organizers as a strategy to enhance learning. Rather, possible tendencies toward relative advantages were noted when subjects constructed graphic organizers as a post-reading activity. . . .

Meta-Analysis and Effect Size

When you read other meta-analyses, you may note that the findings are sometimes reported in terms of *effect sizes.* This is a different index of the potency of the variable under consideration. Effect sizes are standard scores (like z scores). They can be positive or negative and are upper and lower limits (theoretically) of infinity. For practical purposes, however, the normal limits would be ± 3.0. A further discussion of effect sizes (in terms of R^2) is given in chapter 6.

To evaluate a meta-analysis, similar questions to those used for reviews should be asked. However, since meta-analysis is a mathematical procedure, the criteria for inclusion of studies must be more precisely spelled out than in reviews. This is also true for the specification of the variables and the like. In general, meta-analyses demand even more precision than reviews. Moreover, meta-analyses require that there be a large number of studies involving the same variables and similar methodology. These conditions are often not met in many areas of reading and writing research. Consequently, there are few meta-analyses in these areas. This is a relatively new technique. It remains to be seen whether it will become more popular.

Box Scores or Tallies

The *box score* procedure is, perhaps, the simplest procedure to use, even though there are a few cautions to be observed. Ladas (1980) describes the procedure in detail, providing some illustrative examples. The method involves examining a selected set of studies and dividing them into groups: (1) those that answer a specific question yes; (2) those that answer the question no; and (3) those that find no differences between the treatments used in the study.

This is not a commonly used technique in reading research synthesis. However, Ladas (1980) points out that it should be particularly useful in reaching conclusions for applications, where preponderance of evidence is the important element. The value of this method is that it is simpler to use and can be effective in helping to reach a decision about an area of research. He illustrates the technique with examples on the role of note taking in studying. Ladas uses an earlier list of studies (taken from Hartley and Davies 1978). He accepts this as the population of studies to be considered. (These are presented in Table 9–3 and Table 9–4.)

One problem that arises is what to do with those studies that show

Table 9–3
A summary of findings with respect to the question: Does the process of note taking itself aid recall?

Studies indicating yes (N = 17)	Studies indicating no significant difference (N = 16)	Studies indicating no (N = 2)
Jones 1923 (1 study)	Jones 1923 (2 studies)	Peters 1972
Crawford 1925b	Crawford 1925b	Thomas, Aiken, &
(2 studies)	(3 studies)	Shennum 1975
McHenry 1969	Freyberg 1956	(Note 10)
(4 studies)	McClendon 1956	
Berliner 1969	Eisner & Rohde 1959	
Berliner 1971 (Note 6)	Pauk 1963	
Berliner 1972 (Note 7)	MacManaway 1968	
Peters & Harris 1970	Howe 1970a	
DiVesta & Gray 1972	Fisher & Harris 1974a	
DiVesta & Gray 1973	Fisher & Harris 1974b	
(2 studies)	Baker et al. 1974	
Fisher & Harris 1973	(1 study)	
Baker, Baker & Blount	Aiken et al. 1975	
1974 (Note 8)	Carter & Van Matre	
Fairbanks & Costello	1975	
(1977)		

Source: From H. Ladas, Summarizing research: A case study, *Review of Educational Research* 50 (1980): 601. Copyright 1980, American Educational Research Association, Washington, D.C.

no difference. Table 9–5 illustrates Ladas' solution—doing a microanalysis of those studies to see whether a consistent reason for the findings of no difference can be found.

In reaching a conclusion, Ladas suggests that note taking is the best strategy, particularly when coupled with reviewing. An important point is that the findings of no difference should be separated from the negative findings; they should not be evaluated in the same way as a true negative finding on the summarization. Microanalysis is a way of uncovering which of the myriad possible reasons accounts for the lack of differences.

WHAT IF THERE AREN'T ANY RELEVANT STUDIES?

The most ominous nightmare of translating research into practice is that you will find no relevant studies to use. In a literal sense, this is almost always the case. As noted above, we rarely find studies that match the needs of a specific situation or environment. We are almost always in the position of trying to get close with a best approximation or to generalize from studies that are less rigorous or appropriate than is desirable.

Table 9–4
A summary of findings with respect to the question: Does reviewing notes help recall?

Studies indicating yes ($N = 13$)	Studies indicating no significant difference ($N = 3$)	Studies indicating no ($N = 0$)
Crawford 1925b (2 studies)	Fisher & Harris 1974a	
Freyberg 1956	Fisher & Harris 1974b	
Howe 1970a	Peters & Harris 1970	
DiVesta & Gray 1972		
Fisher & Harris 1973		
Hartley & Marshall 1974		
Carter & Van Matre 1975		
Annis & Davis 1977 (Note 9)		
Howe & Godfrey 1977 (4 studies)		

Source: From H. Ladas, Summarizing research: A case study, *Review of Educational Research* 50 (1980): 601. Copyright 1980, American Educational Research Association, Washington, D.C.

If you encounter this situation, you have only one alternative: Make your best guess about what to do, and then proceed to keep close watch on the results of your implementation. If you evaluate performance carefully, you should be able to determine whether your choice was appropriate. In fact, what you have done in this case is to conduct a simple research study. Remember, you must be willing to change the program if it does not produce desired results after a sufficiently long period of time.

Fortunately, it is usually possible to find some research studies or reviews to help us inform our instructional implementations. That is, the lack of a single relevant study is so rare that you need never be concerned about the possibility.

FOLLOWING UP RESEARCH IMPLEMENTATION

After you have reached a decision about instruction on the basis of research and then implemented it, your task is not over. There is still the possibility that what you have settled on will not work because of some unknown or obscure factor or variable. You (and possibly others) may have overlooked something, or you may be dealing with a different population or situation. Once you use research to inform your instructional practice, you must become a researcher, constantly verifying that what you have implemented *really is* instructionally effective.

Table 9–5
A microanalysis of experiments on note taking that resulted in no difference

Assumed Critical Factors	Studies			
	McClendon 1956	Eisner & Rohde 1959	Fisher & Harris 1974a	Fisher & Harris 1974b
Design				
Untreated Control	+	− −	+ +	+ +
Randomization	−	−	+	+
Adequate Power	?	− −	?	?
Variable(s) Tested	E	I	E & R	E & R
Subjects				
Unfamiliar c Treatment Material	?	?	?	?
Unable to ans. items from cues	+	−	?	?
Possess Entry Behavior	+	?	?	?
Possess Aptitude	?	?	?	?
Follow Directions	−	−	?	?
Materials				
Difficulty	?	?	?	?
Average rate, wpm	132	?	?	?
Meaningfulness	?	?	?	?
Length in Minutes	14	30	20	20
Information Density	?	?	?	?
Procedure				
Adequate Instructions	+	− −	+	+
Timing of Review	None	None	Immed.	Immed.
Timing of Test in Days	Immed. & 35			Immed. LTRT
Criterion Measure(s)				
Edumetric Test	−	−	−	−
Test Development	+	−	−	−
K$_{r20}$ or Split-half Reported	+	−	−	−
Total				
Methodological deficiencies	0	3	0	0
Lack of control	3	6	3	3
Explicit control statement omitted	6	7	10	10

Note: (− −) = Methodological deficiencies
   (−) = Lack of control
   (?) = Explicit control statement omitted
   (+) = Explicitly stated control
   (+ +) = Explicitly stated control & good example for future research
   LTRT = Lecture/test/review/test with no delay
   E = encoding; R = review; I = interference
Source: From H. Ladas, Summarizing research: A case study, *Review of Educational Research* 50 (1980): 607. Copyright 1980, American Educational Research Association, Washington, D.C.

Researchers and practitioners have often viewed their roles as mutually exclusive, when they really should be viewed as collaborative. Each brings special knowledge and insight to the question being asked. Together, they can help improve research and instruction in all dimensions. Research should be thought of as a *process* rather than a *product*, engaged in by all educators interested in working toward increased knowledge and improved practice.

REFERENCES

Cohen, J. (1977). *Statistical power analysis for the behavioral sciences* (Rev. ed.). New York: Academic Press.

Cooper, H. (1982). Scientific guidelines for conducting integrative research reviews. *Review of Educational Research, 52,* 291–302.

Gentile, L., Kamil, M., & Blanchard, J. (1983). *Reading research revisited.* Columbus, OH: C. E. Merrill.

Guthrie, J., Seifert, M., & Mosberg, L. (1983). Research synthesis in reading: Topics, audiences, and citation rates. *Reading Research Quarterly, 19,* 16–27.

Jackson G. (1980). Methods for integrative reviews. *Review of Educational Research, 50,* 438–460.

Ladas, H. (1980). Summarizing research: A case study. *Review of Educational Research, 50,* 597–624.

Moore, D., & Readence, J. (1980). A meta-analysis of the effect of graphic organizers on learning from text. In M. Kamil (Ed.), *Perspectives in reading research and instruction.* Washington, D.C.: The National Reading Conference.

Sticht, T., Beck, L., Hauke, R., Kleiman, G., & James, J. (1974). *Auding and reading.* Alexandria, VA: HumRRO (Human Resources Research Organization).

ADDITIONAL READINGS
ON INTEGRATING AND SUMMARIZING RESEARCH

Carver, R. (1978). The case against statistical significance testing. *Harvard Educational Rivew, 48,* 378–399.

Cohen, S., & Hyman, J. (1979). How come so many hypotheses in educational research are supported? (A modest proposal). *Educational Researcher, 8*(11), 12–16.

Curry, J., & Morris, W. (1975). *Searching the professional literature in reading.* Newark, DE: International Reading Association.

Glass, G. (1977). Integrating findings: The meta-analysis of research. *Review of research in education* (Vol. 5). Itasca, IL: Peacock.

Glass, G., McGaw, B., & Smith, M. (1981). *Meta-analysis in social research.* Beverly Hills, CA: Sage Publications.

Guthrie, J. (Ed.) (1984). *Reading: A research retrospective, 1881–1941* (Selections from the William S. Gray collection). Newark, DE: International Reading Association.

Harris, T., & Hodges, R. (Eds.). (1981). *A dictionary of reading and related terms.* Newark, DE: International Reading Association.

Jenkins, J. (1979). Four points to remember: A tetrahedral model of memory experiments. In L. S. Cermak & F. I. M. Craik (Eds.), *Levels of processing in human memory.* Hillsdale, NJ: Erlbaum.

Kerlinger, F. (1977). The influence of research on educational practice. *Educational Researcher, 6,* 5–12.

SOURCES FOR RESEARCH REVIEWS

The following periodicals publish reviews of research in specific areas in education:

Annual Summary of Investigations Relating To Reading. (Published by the International Reading Association.)

Psychological Review. (Published by the American Psychological Association.)

Review of Educational Research. (Published by the American Educational Research Association.)

Yearbook of the National Reading Conference. (Published by the National Reading Conference.)

The following books are collections of reviews on selected topics in reading and writing:

Farr, M. (Ed.). (1982). *Writing: The nature, development, and teaching of written communication* (Vol. 1). Hillsdale, NJ: Erlbaum.

Frederickson, C., & Dominic, J. (Eds.). (1982). *Writing: The nature, development, and teaching of written communication* (Vol. 2). Hillsdale, NJ: Erlbaum.

Gentile, L., Kamil, M., & Blanchard, J. (Eds.). (1983). *Reading research revisited.* Columbus, OH: C. E. Merrill.

Guthrie, J. (Ed.). (1981). *Comprehension and teaching: Research review.* Newark, DE: International Reading Association.

Pearson, P., Barr, R., Kamil, M., & Mosenthal, P. (Eds.). (1984). *Handbook of reading research.* New York: Longman.

Journals that Contain Reading and Writing Research

Abstracts of English Studies
Academic Therapy
Alberta Journal of Educational Research
American Education
American Educational Research Journal
American Journal of Community Psychology
American Journal of Education
American Journal of Psychology
American Journal of Sociology
American Psychologist
Applied Psycholinguistics
Arizona English Bulletin
Australian Journal of Reading
Behavioral Science
Behavioral Science Research
Brain & Language
British Journal of Disorders of Communication
British Journal of Educational Psychology
British Journal of Educational Studies
British Journal of Psychology
British Journal of Sociology of Education
Bulletin of the Orton Society

California Reader
Canadian Journal of Psychology
Child Development
Children's Literature in Education
Cognitive Psychology
Cognitive Science
College Composition and Communication
College English
Colorado Journal of Educational Research
Communication Education
Communication Monographs
Communication Research
Comparative Education
Comparative Education Review
Connecticut English Journal
Contemporary Education
Contemporary Education Review
Contemporary Educational Psychology
Contemporary Psychology
Cortex
CSSEDC Quarterly
Curriculum Inquiry
Developmental Psychology

Discourse Processes

Education

Education and Psychological Measurement

Education Communication and Technology Journal

Educational Psychologist

Educational Psychology

Educational Psychology and Theory

Educational Record

Educational Research

Educational Research Quarterly

Educational Researcher

Educational Review

Educational Studies

Educational Technology

Elementary School Journal

English in Australia

English Education

English Journal

English Language Teaching

Epistle

Harvard Educational Review

High School Journal

Illinois Reading Council Journal

Illinois School Research and Development

International Review of Education

Irish Journal of Education

Journal of the Acoustical Society of America

Journal of Communication

Journal of Communication Disorders

Journal of Curriculum Studies

Journal of Education

Journal of Educational Measurement

Journal of Educational Psychology

Journal of Educational Research

Journal of Educational Thought

Journal of Experimental Child Psychology

Journal of Experimental Education

Journal of Experimental Psychology: General

Journal of Experimental Psychology: Human Perception and Cognition

Journal of Experimental Psychology: Learning, Memory, and Performance

Journal of General Education

Journal of General Psychology

Journal of Genetic Psychology

Journal of Learning Disabilities

Journal of Mental Imagery

Journal of Multilingual and Multicultural Development

Journal of Optometric Vision Development

Journal of Reading

Journal of Reading Behavior

Journal of Research and Development in Education

Journal of Research in Reading

Journal of School Psychology

Journal of Special Education

Journal of Speech and Hearing Disorders

Journal of Speech and Hearing Research

Journal of Teacher Education

Journal of Verbal Learning and Verbal Behavior

Journal of Visual Impairment & Blindness

Kappa Delta Pi Record

Language and Speech

Language Arts

Language in Society

Language Learning

Learning Disabilities Quarterly

Linguistic Inquiry

Linguistics: An Interdisciplinary Journal of the Language Sciences

Media and Methods

Memory and Cognition

Mental Retardation

Merrill-Palmer Quarterly

Michigan Reading Journal

Modern Language Journal

Monographs in Language and Reading Studies

Monographs of the Society for Research in Child Development

National Reading Conference Yearbook

New England Reading Association Journal

North Central Association Quarterly

Ohio Reading Teacher

Peabody Journal of Education

Perception and Psychophysics

Perceptual and Motor Skills

Phi Delta Kappan

Programmed Learning and Educational Technology

Psychological Bulletin

Psychological Record

Psychological Reports

Psychological Review

Psychology

Psychology in the Schools

Quarterly Journal of Experimental Psychology

Quarterly Journal of Speech

Reading

Reading—Canada—Lecture

Reading Education

Reading Education: A Journal for Australian Teachers

Reading Horizons

Reading Improvement

Reading Instruction Journal

Reading Psychology

Reading Research Quarterly

Reading Teacher, The

Reading World

Research in the Teaching of English

Review of Education, The

Review of Educational Research

School Library Journal

School Media Quarterly

Science of Reading

Studies in Language

Tar Heel Reading Journal

Teachers College Record

Teaching Exceptional Children

Theory into Practice

Today's Education

Topics in Language Disorders

Topics in Learning & Learning Disabilities

Urban Education

Visible Language

Vision Research

Wilson Library Bulletin

Written Communication

Critical Values of the Pearson Product-Moment Correlation Coefficient

	Level of significance for a directional (one-tailed) test				
	.05	.025	.01	.005	.0005
	Level of significance for a non-directional (two-tailed) test				
$df = N-2$	.10	.05	.02	.01	.001
1	.9877	.9969	.9995	.9999	1.0000
2	.9000	.9500	.9800	.9900	.9990
3	.8054	.8783	.9343	.9587	.9912
4	.7293	.8114	.8822	.9172	.9741
5	.6694	.7545	.8329	.8745	.9507
6	.6215	.7067	.7887	.8343	.9249
7	.5822	.6664	.7498	.7977	.8982
8	.5494	.6319	.7155	.7646	.8721
9	.5214	.6021	.6851	.7348	.8471
10	.4973	.5760	.6581	.7079	.8233
11	.4762	.5529	.6339	.6835	.8010
12	.4575	.5324	.6120	.6614	.7800
13	.4409	.5139	.5923	.6411	.7603
14	.4259	.4973	.5742	.6226	.7420
15	.4124	.4821	.5577	.6055	.7246
16	.4000	.4683	.5425	.5897	.7084
17	.3887	.4555	.5285	.5751	.6932
18	.3783	.4438	.5155	.5614	.6787
19	.3687	.4329	.5034	.5487	.6652
20	.3598	.4227	.4921	.5368	.6524
25	.3233	.3809	.4451	.4869	.5974
30	.2960	.3494	.4093	.4487	.5541
35	.2746	.3246	.3810	.4182	.5189
40	.2573	.3044	.3578	.3932	.4896
45	.2428	.2875	.3384	.3721	.4648
50	.2306	.2732	.3218	.3541	.4433
60	.2108	.2500	.2948	.3248	.4078
70	.1954	.2319	.2737	.3017	.3799
80	.1829	.2172	.2565	.2830	.3568
90	.1726	.2050	.2422	.2673	.3375
100	.1638	.1946	.2301	.2540	.3211

Note: If the observed value of *r* is *greater than or equal to* the tabulated value for the appropriate level of significance (columns) and degrees of freedom (rows), then reject H_o. The degrees of freedom are the number of pairs of scores minus two, or $N - 2$. the critical values in the table are both + and − for nondirectional (two-tailed) tests.

Source: From Table VII of Fisher & Yates, *Statistical Tables for Biological, Agricultural and Medical Research,* published by Longman Group Ltd., London (previously published by Oliver and Boyd Ltd., Edinburgh) and by permission of the authors and publishers.

Subject Index

abstracting services, 161
abstracts
  Current Index to Journals in Education, 162
  Dissertation Abstracts, 162
  Psychological Abstracts, 161–162
  use in locating research, 161–162
  use in screening research, 24
Academic Learning Time (ALT), 65
achievement tests, 50–51. *See also* tests
ALT. *See* Academic Learning Time
alternate forms reliability, 34. *See also* reliability
alternate hypothesis, 98–99
alternative hypothesis, 98–99, 111
analysis of covariance, 124
  and quasi-experiments, 144–145
anonymity, 49–50
ANOVA, 115, 118, 122–123, 124
  and multiple regression, 132
  and multivariate research, 129, 130–131
applied research, 2–3
archival data, 50–51
Aristotle, 1
attenuation, correction for, 37
attitudinal information, 48–49, 50

balanced position, 6
balancing/counterbalancing extraneous variables, 95
Bartlett-Box, 115
basic research, 2–3
Beginning Teacher Evaluation Study, 65
beta weights, 143–144, 151, 153
between-subjects variables, 116–118

bias
  in complex experimental designs, 113
  in descriptive research data, 56
  influence of researcher, 4–5, 181–182
  in literature searches, 175
  in observation, 50
  in surveys, 49
biserial coefficient correlation method, 33
bivariate correlation, descriptive research, 52
Books in Print, 163
bottom-up position, 5
box scores, 163, 178–179

canonical correlation, 130
case histories, 7–8, 63, 76
causation, 6–8
  and correlational research, 29, 44–45
  and descriptive research, 66
  and experimental research, 91, 107, 144, 146
  and multiple regression, 144–145
  and multivariate research, 107, 136, 137, 144
  and nonexperiments, 145–146
  and quasi-experiments, 92, 144, 146
  and research approaches, 146
  and simple experimental designs, 91, 107
  and variance, 107
Child Development, 16
CIJE. *See Current Index to Journals in Education*
cloze test performance, 145
coefficient of determination, 136

190

naturalistic inquiry, 71
naturalistic orientation
  basic theory, 16
  data analysis, 19–21
  data collection, 17–18, 19
  data reporting, 17–18, 19
  report structure, 22–23
negative correlation, 27
Newman-Keuls test, 111
nonexperiments, 145–146
nonlinear relationships, 32–33
nonparametric tests, and complex
    experimental designs, 124
note taking, role in studying, 178–179
null hypotheses, 4
  and research questions, 4
  and simple experimental designs, 98–99
  and statistical analysis, 110–111

objective information (from surveys), 48–
    49, 50
observational study, 59–60
  data collection, 50, 54, 66
  and ethnographic research, 73, 76
  subject reaction to, 50, 60, 97
one-way analysis of variance, 110–111
operational definition, 94
opinion information (from surveys), 48–49
oral language comprehension, 165–175
oral reading, 54–55, 145–146
order effects, and multiple regression, 147–
    148

partial factorial designs, 123
participant structures, reading instruction,
    87–88
passage dependence, 35–37
passage organization, 145
path analysis, and multivariate research,
    130
Pearson product correlations, 30, 40–42,
    43–44, 188–189
Phi coefficient correlational method, 33
Piagetian theory, 140
point biserial correlation method, 33
  and synthesizing research, 176–177
population (in research report)
  and complex experimental designs, 112–
    113
  definition, 53
  and simple experimental designs, 96–97,
    99
positive correlation, 26–27
practitioners, influence on research, 4–5,
    181–182
predicted variance, and multivariate
    research, 135–137
principle components factor analysis. See
    factor analysis
print awareness,, 133–136

Procedures (section of research report). See
    also research report, structure of
  and complex experimental designs, 113–
    115
  and descriptive research, 55
Psychological Abstracts (PA), 161–163. See also
    abstracts
Psychological Review, 162
Pyrczak indices, 35–37

quasi-experimental research, 10
  and causation, 92, 144, 146
  definition, 144
  and descriptive research, 52
  and multiple regression, 144
questionnaires, 48–49, 55, 66

random sampling, 53–54
randomization, 144, 147
reader/writer/learner variables, 11
readers
  abilities of, 64, 131–132
  beginning, 31–32, 65, 131–132
  good vs. poor, 92, 142–143
  high school, 131
  inference abilities, 112–115
  NAEP study, 64
  predicting ability, 131–132
  and spelling achievement, 136
reading and writing research. See research
    orientations; research questions;
    research reports, reading of; research
    reports, structure of
reading comprehension, 43–44
  cognitive perspectives, 119–120
  instruction, 56–64
  learning process, 142–144
  and oral language comprehension, 165–
    175
  standardized tests, 148–149
  verbal processing abilities, 138–143
  and vocabulary, 135–136
reading instruction
  of comprehension, 56–64
  curriculum, 65
  descriptive studies of, 65
  flowcharting, 145
  oral reading, 54–55
  participant structures, 87–88
  poor vs. good readers, 87
  remedial, 65
  test scores, 50–51
  theory of reading process, 5–6
  types of, 65
recall of written prose, 100–106
regression analyses, 8
regression, stepwise, 140–143
reliability
  alternate forms, 34
  and correlation, 33–37

single-/small-N design, 9–10
skills position, 5
Skinner, B. F., 9
social competence, school, 74–75
Social SciSearch (ISI), 162–163
Sociological Abstracts (SA), 162–163. *See also* abstracts
Spearman rho, 31
split-half reliability, 34
standardized tests, 148–149. *See also* tests
statistical analyses
    cautions regarding, 124
    and complex experimental designs, 109, 110–111
statistical inferences, 53–54, 55, 58
statistical significance, and complex experimental designs, 124–125
stepwise regressions, 140–143
stratified random sampling, 53–54
subjects-to-measures ratio, 149–150
subsequent test procedures, 118–119
Summary of Investigations Relating to Reading, 162
summary tables, 121–123
surveys, 48–49, 54, 55, 66, 154
symposium proceedings, 161

t-ratio, 176–177
t-test, 28, 32
    and complex experimental designs, 124
    and simple experimental designs, 98, 99
    statistical analyses, 110–111
    subsequent tests, 111–112
tallies, 163, 178–179
tape recordings, 87
test-retest reliability, 34
tests
    and correlation, 33–40
    design and development of, 132
    and factor analysis, 132
    length of, 34
    objective, 50–51, 54
    reliability of, 25, 34
    standardized, 148–149
    validity of, 25, 38–40
tests of significance, 142–144
tetrachoric correlational method, 33
text dimensions, effects of, 112–115
Thesaurus of ERIC Descriptors, 162
theses, unpublished, 175. *See also* dissertations
time series design, 9–10
top-down position, 5–6
translators, influence on research, 5
triangulation, 76
Tuinman indices, 35, 37
Tukey procedure, 111
two-group design, 8–9, 97, 100–106, 110

validity
    and data collection, 54
    and descriptive research, 60

determination of, 160–161
and ethnographic research, 76
and integrative reviews, 175
and simple experimental designs, 99–100
types of, 99–100
variables
    between-subjects, 116–118
    confounded, 96–97, 100
    definition of, 94–95
    dependent, 26, 100, 130–131
    entry order, 140–142
    extraneous, 147–148
    independent, 26, 100, 115–118, 130–131
    interactions, 109, 119–120
    manipulation of, 10, 25, 91–92, 115–118, 145–146
    MANOVA, 152–153
    and multiple regression, 137–142
    and multivariate research, 130–131, 137–142
    nonmanipulable, 42–44
    prediction of, 44
    reducing sets, 131–132
    repeated-measure, 117
    and simple experimental designs, 91–92, 94–95
    simplifying sets, 131–132
    types of, 11, 94–95, 129
    within-subject, 117–118
variance
    accounting for, 132–144
    communality statistics, 154–155
    and multiple regression, 137–140
    and multivariate research, 135–140
    one-way analysis of, 110–111
    prediction of, 135–137
variance accounted for, 135–137
variance explained, 135–137
verbal processing abilities, 138–143
verbal strategies, home and community settings, 77–86
video tape, 17, 23, 76
vocabulary, and reading comprehension, 135–136

Wilcoxon test, 124
Wilks lambda, 152–153
within-subject variables, 117–118
word recognition, 43–44
writing ability, 116
    essay composition, 121–123
    evaluation of, 131
    NAEP study, 52, 64
    of young children, 17–19, 20, 22
writing instruction, 1, 65
writing process, 1, 5, 6, 66
writing research. *See* research orientations; research questions; research reports, reading of; research reports, structure of

Z-tests, 28

Author Index

Rogers, B., 49
Rowe, D., 124
Rowls, M., 50–51
Ruddell, R. B., 2, 48
Rumelhart, D., 6
Rupley, W. H., 48
Ryan, E. B., 31–32

Samuels, S. J., 5, 43–44
Scardamalia, M., 2
Schallert, D., 119–120
Schultz, J., 74–75, 86
Schutz, A., 71
Schwartz, R., 117, 118–119
Scollon, R., 76
Scollon, S. B. K., 76
Scribner, S., 145
Searfoss, L. W., 47
Seifert, M., 162–163
Shanahan, T., 65, 131, 145, 150
Shatz, 82
Shaunessy, M. P., 1
Shavelson, R., 111
Simons, H., 87, 153
Singer, H., 2
Skinner, B. F., 9
Smith, F., 5
Snow, 80
Spindler, G., 77–86
Stack, 82
Stallings, J., 65
Stanley, J. C., 8, 38, 99, 123

Stewart, M. F., 131
Sticht, T., 165–175
Sullivan, H. J., 8

Teale, W. H., 154
Thorndike, R., 34, 38
Tierney, R. J., 40–42, 153
Tobin, A. W., 145
Toms-Bronowski, S., 132
Tuinman, J., 50–51

Vosniadou, S., 116–117
Vygotsky, 31

Walberg, H. J., 131, 149
Wallat, C., 86
Ward, 82
Warriner, J. E., 5
Weber, M., 71
Weinreich, 101
Weintraub, 80
Williamson, M., 116
Witte, S. P., 132
Wixson, K., 125
Woolfson, W., 112–114
Wundt, W., 1

Young, 82

Zaharias, J. A., 132
Zigmond, N., 146